GW00647992

Heart speak

Visit that touched the so

It is appropriate to describe the papal visit 2010 as a landmark moment for our Catholic Community; not only was the visit heavy with powerful moments of history and celebration, but the perception of our Church and of our relationship to wider society was transformed – not least for ourselves as Catholics.

Most of us went into this visit have been battered and beleaguered for some time by certain elements of society and the media determined to consign our faith, and faith in general, to the sidelines, and by scandals within our own Church.

Pope Benedict clearly recognised that concern; as early as his first interview on the incoming papal flight he confronted squarely our position and responsibilities concerning the horror of sexual abuse, a theme he revisited bravely and uncompromisingly several times during his visit.

On politics, too, he stressed that Catholic Social Teaching offers a perfect and long-established ethical blueprint, stretching back to Leo XIII and beyond, for everything from corporate finance to social care and the dignity of the human person.

As you will read here, in all of his speeches he presented a wonderfully rounded, broad summary of the Catholic faith and its concerns, defying the secular perception that we are a narrow faith with equally narrow preoccupations.

On a more personal level he also buried the epithet of "God's Rottweiler", revealing himself instead to be a humble man of the people, deep of faith and principles, yet touchingly moved by the warmth of others, especially of the young people he met.

There's no doubt he also enjoyed thoroughly what must have been a visit he faced with some degree of nervousness; for that we should put on record a huge note of thanks to everyone who made the visit possible and such a huge success, especially the members of the clergy, hierarchy and other Church organisations who worked so tirelessly behind the scenes.

I'm sure they would also want to join us in offering immense gratitude and thanks to countless Catholics everywhere, who not only gave the Holy Father such a warm and loving reception, but who demonstrated very publicly that the Catholic faith remains both vibrant and eloquent, and that the ancient Christian foundations of these blessed islands have not been in any way diminished in recent times.

There has been such interest in the words spoken by the Holy Father and others during this historic visit, that we felt it important to reproduce them in a resource that could be used in the months and years to come, both for personal inspiration and as a basis for more formal study and meditation.

It is very much my hope that these critically important statements will contribute to a renewed enthusiasm and sense of self-confidence within our Church and beyond, for the creation of a society based on sound moral and social principles, and one that recognises the dignity of the human person at all stages of life.

Joseph Kelly
Managing Director
Universe Media Group Ltd

© Mazur/www.thepapalvisit.org.uk

As is traditional at the start of Apostolic Journeys, Pope Benedict XVI held a mid-flight press conference with journalists accompanying him on his four-day visit to the United Kingdom. Here is a Vatican Radio translation of the question and answer session:

Q. – Your Holiness, welcome among us and thank you for being available for our questions. We have a group of 70 journalists present here from different parts of the world. Of course some have come especially from the UK to join our group for the flight. As usual, in recent days my colleagues have given me several questions for consideration in this initial conversation, the beginning of a long-awaited and challenging journey, which we hope will be truly beautiful. I chose a series of questions, from among those that were submitted, and I will ask them in Italian so as not to tax you too much. My colleagues will help those who are not familiar with Italian, to understand. The first question: during the preparation for this journey there have been contrary discussions and positions. The country has a past tradition of a strong anti-Catholic position. Are you concerned about how you will be received?

A. - Firstly, good day to you all and I wish you a good journey. I must say that I'm not worried, because when I went to France I was told: "This will be a most anti-clerical country with strong anti-clerical currents and with a minimum of faithful." When I went to the Czech Republic it was said: "This is the most non-religious country in Europe and even the most anti-clerical". So Western countries, all have, each in their own specific way, according to their own history, strong anti-clerical or anti-Catholic currents, but they always also have a strong

presence of faith. So in France and the Czech Republic I saw and experienced a warm welcome by the Catholic community, a strong attention from agnostics, who, however, are searching, who want to know, to find the values that advance humanity and they were very careful to see if they could hear something from me in this respect, and tolerance

Pope Benedict XVI waves to journalists aboard a plane on the way to Edinburgh, Scotland, (September 16th). Standing with him, from left, is Mgr. Georg Ganswein, the Pope's personal secretary; Cardinal Tarcisio Bertone, the Vatican secretary of state; and Jesuit Father Federico Lombardi, the Vatican spokesman. © Catholic News Service.

and respect for those who are anti-Catholic. Of course Britain has its own history of anti-Catholicism, this is obvious, but is also a country with a great history of tolerance. And so I'm sure on the one hand, there will be a positive reception from Catholics, from believers in general, and attention from those who seek as we move forward in our time, mutual respect and tolerance. Where there is anti-Catholicism I will go forward with great courage and joy.

Q. - The UK, like many other Western countries - there is an issue that you have already touched on in the first answer – it is considered a secular country. There is a strong atheist movement, even for cultural reasons. However, there are also signs that religious faith, particularly in Jesus Christ, is still alive on a personal level. What can this mean for Catholics and Anglicans? Can anything be done to make the Church as an institution more credible and attractive to everyone?

A. - I would say that a Church that seeks to be particularly attractive is already on the wrong path,

because the Church does not work for her own ends, she does not work to increase numbers and thus power. The Church is at the service of another: she serves, not for herself, not to be a strong body, rather she serves to make the proclamation of Jesus Christ accessible, the great truths and great forces of love, reconciling love that appeared in this figure and that always comes from the presence of Jesus Christ. In this regard, the Church does not seek to be attractive in and of herself, but must be transparent for Jesus Christ and to the extent that she is not out for herself, as a strong and powerful body in the world, that wants power, but is simply the voice of another, she becomes truly transparent for the great figure of Christ and the great truth that he has brought to humanity. The power of love, in this moment one listens, one accepts. The Church should not consider herself, but help to consider the other and she herself must see and speak of the other. In this sense, I think, both Anglicans and Catholics have the same simple task, the same direction to take. If both Anglicans and Catholics see that the other is not out for themselves but are tools of Christ, children of the Bridegroom, as St John says, if both carry out the priorities of Christ and not their own, they will come together, because at that time the priority of Christ unites them and they are no longer competitors seeking the greatest numbers, but are united in our commitment to the truth of Christ who comes into this world and so they find each other in a genuine and fruitful ecumenism.

Q. - Thank you Your Holiness. A third question. As is well known and as was also highlighted by recent surveys, the sexual abuse scandal has shaken the confidence of the faithful in the Church. How do you think you can help restore that trust?

A. - First, I must say that these revelations have been a shock for me, not only a great sadness. It is difficult to understand how this perversion of the priestly ministry was possible. The priest at the time of ordination, after having prepared for this moment for years, says yes to Christ, to be his voice, his mouth, his hands and serve Him with his whole life, so that the Good Shepherd who loves and helps and guides to the truth is present in the world. How a man who has done this and said this may also fall into this perversion is difficult to understand. It is a great sadness, a sadness that even the authority of the Church has not been sufficiently vigilant and not fast or decided enough in taking the necessary measures. Because of all of this, we are in a time of repentance, humility, and renewed sincerity. As I wrote to the Irish bishops, I think we now realise it's a time of penance, a time to renew and relearn humility with complete sincerity. Regarding the victims, I would say there are three important things. Our first interest is for the victims: how can we repair >

the damage done? What can we do to help these people overcome this trauma, to regain their life and rediscover confidence in the message of Christ? Care, commitment to victims is the first priority, with material, psychological, spiritual aid. Second, the problem of the guilty persons. The just punishment is exclusion from all possibilities of access to young people because we know that this is a disease and free will does not work where there is disease. So we have to protect these people against themselves and find ways to help them, protect them against themselves and exclude them from any access to young people. The third point is prevention in education, in the choice of candidates for the priesthood to be so careful that, as much as humanly possible, we exclude future cases. And I would now also like to thank the British bishops for their attention and co-operation with both the See of St Peter and with public bodies. It seems to me that the British bishops have done a great job in their attention to the sensitivity of the victims and the law and I am very grateful to them for this.

Q. – Your Holiness, the figure of Cardinal Newman is obviously very significant: you have made an exception for Cardinal Newman to preside over the beatification. Do you think that his memory will help to overcome divisions between Anglicans and Catholics? What are the aspects of his personality which you would like to give stronger emphasis to?

A. - Cardinal Newman is mainly, on the one hand, a modern man, who took on all of the problems of modernity, he experienced the problem of agnosticism, the impossibility of knowing God, of believing; a man who throughout his life was on a journey, a journey to let himself be transformed by the truth, in a search of great sincerity and great willingness, to learn more, to find and to accept the path to true life. This modernity of his inner-being and life points to the modernity of his faith: it is not a faith in the formulas of a bygone age, it is a most personal form of faith, lived, suffered, found through a long process of renewal and conversion. He is a man of great culture who on the one hand participates in our sceptical culture of today, in the question: "Can we understand something certain about the truth of man, of the human being, or not? And how can we arrive at the convergence of the verisimilitude?". A man who, on the other hand, with a great knowledge of the culture of the Church Fathers, he studied and renewed the internal genesis of the faith, thus acknowledging his figure and his inner constitution, he is a man of great spirituality, a great humanism, a man of prayer, of a deep relationship with God and a relationship with himself, and therefore also of a deep relationship with the other men of his and our time. So I would say these three elements: the modernity of his

existence, with all the doubts and problems of our existence today, his great culture, knowledge of the great cultural treasures of mankind, his constant quest for the truth, continuous renewal and spirituality: spiritual life, life with God, give this man an exceptional greatness for our time. Therefore, he is a figure of Doctor of the Church for us, for all and also a bridge between Anglicans and Catholics.

Q. - And one last question, this visit is considered a state visit – this is how it has been qualified. What does this mean for relations between the Holy See and the United Kingdom? Are there are major points of common accord, particularly given the great challenges of today's world?

A. - I am very grateful to Her Majesty, Queen Elizabeth II, who wanted to give this visit the rank of a state visit and who expressed the public nature of this visit and also the common responsibility of politics and religion for the future of the continent, for the future of humanity: the large, shared responsibility so that the values that create justice and politics and which come from religion, share the journey in our time. Of course, the fact that legally it is a state visit, does not make this visit a political matter, because if the Pope is head of state, this is just an instrument to ensure the independence of his message and public nature of his work as pastor.

In this sense, the state visit is substantially and essentially a pastoral visit, a visit in the responsibility of the faith for which the Supreme Pontiff, the Pope, exists. Of course, the character of a state visit focuses attention on the converging interests of politics and religion. Politics is essentially designed to ensure justice and with justice, freedom, but justice is a moral value, a religious value, and so faith, the proclamation of the Gospel, connects with politics in justice and here common interests are also born. Britain has a great experience and a great record in combating the evils of this time, misery, poverty, disease, drugs and all these fights against misery, poverty, slavery, abuse of man, drugs ... are also the goals of the faith, because they are the aims of the humanisation of man, so that the image of God be restored against the destruction and devastation. Another common task is the commitment to world peace and the ability to live peace, peace education and establish the virtues that make man capable of peace. And, finally, an essential element of peace is the dialogue of religions, tolerance, openness to one another and this is a deep aim both of Britain, as a society, and of the Catholic faith: to be open to the outside world, open to dialogue, in this way to be open to truth and the common path of humanity and to rediscovering the values that are the foundation of our humanism! ■

Pope urges people of Great Britain to preserve Christian tradition

Arriving in Scotland on the first leg of a four-day visit to Great Britain, Pope Benedict XVI appealed for preservation of the country's long Christian tradition and warned against 'aggressive' forms of secularism and atheism.

"Your forefathers' respect for truth and justice, for mercy and charity come to you from a faith that remains a mighty force for good in your kingdom, to the great benefit of Christians and non-Christians alike," the Pope said at a reception with Queen Elizabeth II and more than 400 distinguished guests at Holyroodhouse in Edinburgh, the Scottish capital.

In an unusual courtesy gesture, the Queen sent her husband, Prince Philip, to greet the Pope when he arrived at the Edinburgh airport after a two-hour flight from Rome. The Pope looked eager to begin his busy programme in Britain, and on the plane he told reporters he felt confident the country would give him a respectful reception – despite differences with some critics of religion.

Edinburgh welcomed the 83-year-old Pope with a display of enthusiasm and Scottish tradition, including a parade, bagpipe bands and tartans designed especially for the visit. It was his first visit as pope to Britain and the first time the country has hosted a pope since 1982, when Pope John Paul II toured England, Scotland and Wales for six days.

Pope Benedict was being hosted on an official state visit, and British authorities pulled out all the stops at Holyroodhouse, a former Augustinian monastery that now serves as the Queen's official residence in Scotland.

The Pope removed his white zucchetto from his head and held it close to his chest as a military band played *God Save the Queen* after having played the Vatican anthem. The Guard of Honour gave the Pope a royal salute in the courtyard of the palace, then the Pope and the Queen held a private meeting and exchanged gifts.

The two moved out onto the palace grounds to a giant marquee, a tent-like structure where hundreds of government and cultural invitees listened to their speeches.

Afterward, the Queen introduced the Pope to a long line of government officials and religious leaders. Among the first was British Deputy Prime Minister Nick Clegg, a declared atheist and the youthful leader of the Liberal Democrats.

The Pope's arrival coincided with St Ninian's Day, marking the feast of Scotland's first saint and evangeliser. Traditional celebrations in honour of the fourth-century saint were resurrected this year, including a parade featuring the harmonic drone of more than 1,000 bagpipe players.

The parade concluded with the Pope's passage in his popemobile. Thousands of schoolchildren lined the parade route and cheered the Pope, who was wearing his new tartan scarf over his shoulders. The bagpipers and drummers who had led the parade stepped to the footpaths and played as the Pope went by.   >

Pope Benedict XVI greets Cardinal Keith O'Brien as he arrives in Edinburgh, Scotland, to begin the first papal state visit to the UK. Also pictured is the Duke of Edinburgh (centre).
© PA Photos.

"Your forefathers' respect for truth and justice, for mercy and charity come to you from a faith that remains a mighty force for good in your kingdom, to the great benefit of Christians and non-Christians alike."

1. The Pope and Her Majesty the Queen exchanged gifts at the start of the state visit. The Pope is pictured looking at his gift, a facsimile of 85 drawings by Hans Holbein the Younger. © PA Photos.

2. Pope Benedict XVI removes his zucchetto during the National Anthem. © PA Photos.

3. Deputy Prime Minister Nick Clegg welcomes Pope Benedict XVI on his arrival at the Palace of Holyroodhouse. © PA Photos.

4. Pope Benedict XVI wears a shawl made of the St Ninian's Day tartan, a special plaid designed for the pontiff's trip to Scotland, while traveling along a street in Edinburgh. © Catholic News Service.

5. Pope Benedict XVI rides in the popemobile down Edinburgh's Princes Street. © PA Photos.

More than 150 protesters were also present, but did not disrupt the Pope's visit or the celebration of the crowds who came out to welcome him.

After the parade, the Pope was treated to a traditional Scottish lunch at the residence of Cardinal Keith O'Brien of St Andrews and Edinburgh; the menu featured 'haggis' – a dish featuring chopped and spiced organ meat from sheep placed in a sheep's stomach and cooked. ■

The Queen's speech to Pope Benedict

Palace of Holyroodhouse, Edinburgh, Thursday, 16th September 2010

Your Holiness,

I am delighted to welcome you to the United Kingdom, and particularly to Scotland, on your first visit as Pope. I recall with great pleasure the memorable pastoral visit of the late Pope John Paul II to this country in 1982. I also have vivid memories of my four visits to the Vatican, and of meeting some of your predecessors on other occasions. I am most grateful to them for receiving, over the years, a number of members of my family with such warm hospitality.

Much has changed in the world during the nearly 30 years since Pope John Paul's visit. In this country, we deeply appreciate the involvement of the Holy See in the dramatic improvement in the situation in Northern Ireland. Elsewhere the fall of totalitarian regimes across central and eastern Europe has allowed greater freedom for hundreds of millions of people. The Holy See continues to have an important role in international issues, in support of peace and development and in addressing common problems like poverty and climate change.

Your Holiness, your presence here today reminds us of our common Christian heritage, and of the Christian contribution to the encouragement of world peace, and to the economic and social development of the less prosperous countries of the world. We are all aware of the special contribution of the Roman Catholic Church particularly in its ministry to the poorest and most deprived members of society, its care for the homeless and for the education provided by its extensive network of schools.

Religion has always been a crucial element in national identity and historical self-consciousness. This has made the relationship between the different faiths a fundamental factor in the necessary co-operation within and between nation states. It is, therefore, vital to encourage a greater mutual and respectful understanding. We know from experience that through committed dialogue, old suspicions can be transcended and a greater mutual trust established.

I know that reconciliation was a central theme in the life of Cardinal John Henry

© PA Photos.

Newman, for whom you will be holding a Mass of Beatification on Sunday. A man who struggled with doubt and uncertainty, his contribution to the understanding of Christianity continues to influence many. I am pleased that your visit will also provide an opportunity to deepen the relationship between the Roman Catholic Church and the established Church of England and the Church of Scotland.

Your Holiness, in recent times you have said that 'religions can never become vehicles of hatred, that never by invoking the name of God can evil and violence be justified'. Today, in this country, we stand united in that conviction. We hold that freedom to worship is at the core of our tolerant and democratic society.

On behalf of the people of the United Kingdom I wish you a most fruitful and memorable visit. ∎

Official Pope Benedict XVI Commemorative Set of Six Spoons

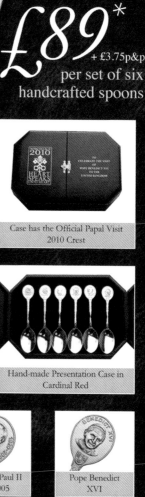

yours for just

£89*

+ £3.75p&p
per set of six
handcrafted spoons

Celebrate the September visit of our Holy Father Pope Benedict XVI with this expertly crafted commemorative spoon set.

Pope Benedict XVI visited the United Kingdom in September 2010, in what was the first papal UK visit since that of John Paul II in 1982. Remember this momentous occasion with this incredible set of six spoons, adorned with memorable popes of grace and humility.

Ornately decorated and presented in a beautiful handmade leatherette case, each spoon is coated in gold. Every spoon depicts a distinguished pope, from St Peter to Benedict XVI, and combines expert craftsmanship with aesthetic beauty.

Each case is emblazoned with a gold embossed papal crest and commemorative text. You can own this highly desirable piece of history for just £89.

* For Sterling Silver or 9 Carat Gold prices please enquire. Gold and Silver spoon sets will be presented in a specially made Black Leatherette Presentation Case with purple lining.

Case has the Official Papal Visit 2010 Crest

Hand-made Presentation Case in Cardinal Red

St Peter
1BC-AD87

St Leo the Great
400-461

St Pius X
1835-1914

Pope John XXIII
1881-1963

Pope John Paul II
1920-2005

Pope Benedict
XVI

How to order

Visit: www.vaughtons.com • Call: 0121 554 9817 / 0121 554 0032
Post: Vaughtons, 16 Well Street, Birmingham B19 3BJ

Please send a cheque for £92.75 made payable to Vaughtons with your name, delivery address, telephone number and "Papal Spoon Set Offer" clearly marked on the reverse.

Since 1819, Vaughtons has been synonymous in the art of commemorative spoon manufacture. Using techniques developed over almost 200 years we are able to offer you this quite superb collection. This collection has been designed by our artist Peter C. who has designed and created many famous works of art throughout the commemorating world. Each spoon is marked with the Vaughtons stamp.

Pope Benedict's speech to The Queen

Palace of Holyroodhouse, Edinburgh, Thursday, 16th September 2010

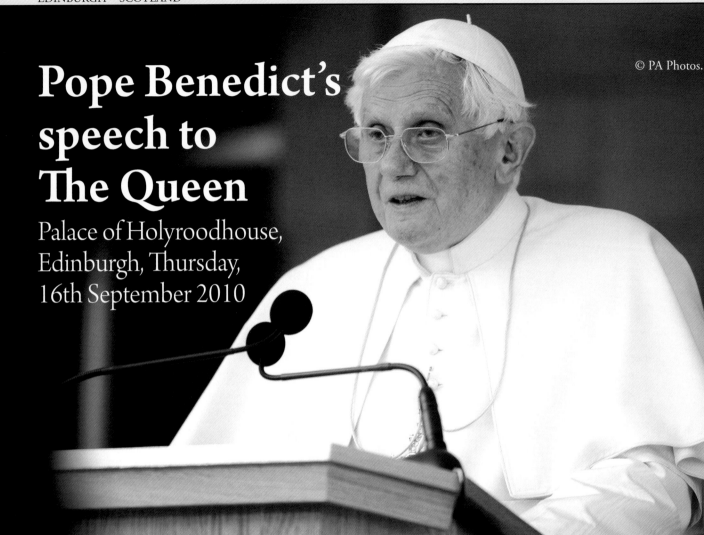

© PA Photos.

Your Majesty,

Thank you for your gracious invitation to make an official visit to the United Kingdom and for your warm words of greeting on behalf of the British people. In thanking Your Majesty, allow me to extend my own greetings to all the people of the United Kingdom and to hold out a hand of friendship to each one.

It is a great pleasure for me to start my journey by saluting the members of the Royal Family, thanking in particular His Royal Highness the Duke of Edinburgh for his kind welcome to me at Edinburgh Airport. I express my gratitude to Your Majesty's present and previous Governments and to all those who worked with them to make this occasion possible, including Lord Patten and former Secretary of State Murphy. I would also like to acknowledge with deep appreciation the work of the All-Party Parliamentary Group on the Holy See, which has contributed greatly to strengthening the friendly relations existing between the Holy See and the United Kingdom.

As I begin my visit to the United Kingdom in Scotland's historic capital city, I greet in a special way First Minister Salmond and the representatives of the Scottish Parliament. Just like the Welsh and Northern Ireland Assemblies, may the Scottish Parliament grow to be an expression of the fine traditions and distinct culture of the Scots and strive to serve their best interests in a spirit of solidarity and concern for the common good.

The name of Holyroodhouse, Your Majesty's official residence in Scotland, recalls the "Holy Cross" and points to the deep Christian roots that are still present in every layer of British life. The monarchs of England and Scotland have been Christians from very early times and include outstanding saints like Edward the Confessor and Margaret of Scotland. As you know, many of them consciously exercised their sovereign duty in the light of the Gospel, and in this way shaped the nation for good at the deepest level. As a result, the Christian message has been an integral part of the language, thought and culture of the peoples of these islands for more than a thousand years. Your forefathers' respect for truth and justice, for mercy and charity come to you from a faith that remains a mighty force for good in your kingdom, to the great benefit of Christians and non-Christians alike.

We find many examples of this force for good throughout Britain's long history. Even in comparatively recent times, due to figures like William Wilberforce and David Livingstone, Britain intervened directly to stop the international slave trade. Inspired by faith, women like Florence Nightingale served the poor and the sick and set new standards in healthcare that were subsequently copied everywhere. John Henry Newman, whose beatification I will celebrate shortly, was one of many British Christians of his age whose goodness, eloquence and action were a credit to their countrymen and women. These, and many people like them, were inspired by a deep faith born and nurtured in these islands.

Even in our own lifetime, we can recall how Britain and her leaders stood against a Nazi tyranny that wished to eradicate God from society and denied our common humanity to many, especially the Jews, who were thought unfit to live. I also recall the regime's attitude to Christian pastors and religious who spoke the truth in love, opposed the Nazis and paid for that opposition with their lives. As we reflect on the sobering lessons of the atheist extremism of the 20th century, let us never forget how the exclusion of God, religion and virtue from public life leads ultimately to a truncated vision of man and of society and thus to a "reductive vision of the person and his destiny" (Caritas in Veritate, 29).

Sixty-five years ago, Britain played an essential role in forging the post-war international consensus which favoured the establishment of the United Nations and ushered in a hitherto unknown period of peace and prosperity in Europe. In more recent years, the international community has followed closely events in Northern Ireland which have led to the signing of the Good Friday Agreement and the devolution of powers to the Northern Ireland Assembly. Your Majesty's Government and the Government of Ireland, together with the political, religious and civil leaders of Northern Ireland, have helped give birth to a peaceful resolution of the conflict there. I encourage everyone involved to continue to walk courageously together on the path marked out for them towards a just and lasting peace.

Looking abroad, the United Kingdom remains a key figure politically and economically on the international stage. Your Government and people are the shapers of ideas that still have an impact far beyond the British Isles. This places upon them a particular duty to act wisely for the common good. Similarly, because their opinions reach such a wide audience, the British media have a graver responsibility than most and a greater opportunity to promote the peace of nations, the integral development of peoples and the spread of authentic human rights. May all Britons continue to live by the values of honesty, respect and fair-mindedness that have won them the esteem and admiration of many.

Today, the United Kingdom strives to be a modern and multicultural society. In this challenging enterprise, may it always maintain its respect for those traditional values and cultural expressions that more aggressive forms of secularism no longer value or even tolerate. Let it not obscure the Christian foundation that underpins its freedoms; and may that patrimony, which has always served the nation well, constantly inform the example your Government and people set before the two billion members of the Commonwealth and the great family of English-speaking nations throughout the world.

May God bless Your Majesty and all the people of your realm. Thank you. ∎

The crowd cheered the 83-year-old pontiff when he arrived at Bellahouston Park, just after a local police bagpipe band played *Amazing Grace*. The crowd had already been warmed up by Susan Boyle, the Scottish singing sensation *(see below)*, who said performing at the papal Mass was the fulfilment of a lifelong dream.

The crowds welcomed the Pope enthusiastically, cheering and waving large yellow and white Vatican flags and large blue and white Scottish flags. He drove through the crowd in the popemobile before Mass, stopping to bless a baby held up by security guards. A Polish woman living in Glasgow said she will "never forget" the moment the Pope kissed her baby girl, Maria Tyszczak, aged 11 months *(see above)*. The girl's mother, Marzena *(inset)*, a 23-year-old cleaner, said: "It was a wonderful moment. I just saw the Pope stop, the guy passed my daughter to the Pope, and I just cried, cried, cried. I will never forget this."

Those attending the Mass had to be in place hours before the Pope arrived. Waiting for the liturgy to begin, they cheered wildly after Boyle sang *How Great Thou Art*.
The crowd was also treated to songs by Michelle McManus *(see far right)*, the 2003 winner of Britain's *Pop Idol* and now host of a morning television programme. ■

PICTURES: PA Photos

Archbishop Conti's welcome message to the Pope

Bellahouston Park, Glasgow, Thursday, 16th September 2010

Pic: © Mazur/www.papalvisit.org.uk

Most Holy Father, Praised be Jesus Christ!

Welcome to Glasgow, entitled by one of your predecessors *Specialis Filia Romanae Ecclesiae - the Special Daughter of the Roman Church.* Welcome to Scotland, to the whole of which another of your predecessors extended that coveted title.

Welcome to the United Kingdom, whose monarch earlier today in the name of all its citizens welcomed you. We, Holy Father, echo that welcome; we form a community of faith obedient to the Gospel, which has been preached in these islands for over 15 centuries - before the land to our south became England, and that on which you stand Scotland.

You come to us on the actual feast of our first-named missionary St Ninian, who, according to a reliable tradition, received his education in Rome and came back ordained to proclaim the Gospel of Christ and to establish His Church.

From Rome also came St Augustine, sent by Pope Gregory the Great, your predecessor, whose arrival in Kent coincided with the death on the Holy Island of Iona of St Columba, who, with his fellow Irish missionaries, evangelised our Scottish Highlands and Islands. Already a British missionary had taken the faith from these shores to those of Ireland whose citizens recognise in St Patrick their great apostle.

Monastic life flourished in our lands, giving us such great saints as Aidan of Lindisfarne and the Venerable Bede.

Centuries later, at the time of the Reformation, devoted men and women were martyred on account of their faith. In this very city St John Ogilvie was hanged for his allegiance to the Holy See. Holy Father, in addition to St Andrew its patron, Scotland holds dear the memory of a saintly queen, Margaret, whose son David revived the ancient bishoprics. In England, and well beyond, men and women admire Thomas More, Chancellor of the Realm, who suffered death for obedience to his conscience; while another great Englishman whom your holiness means to beatify, John Henry Newman, preached on the primacy of a conscience responsive to the truth.

Welcome, Holy Father, to this spot where your venerable predecessor John Paul II challenged us "for the future to walk hand in hand", and whereby we have created a warmth of friendship with which Christians throughout the United Kingdom embrace you today in your visit to the lands we love and the communities we serve.

Finally we welcome you, Holy Father, as the Servant of Christ Jesus and the Servant of the Servants of God.

Cead Mille Failte: A hundred thousand welcomes! ∎

At Mass in Scotland, Pope urges Catholics to show faith publicly

Homily: Bellahouston Park, Glasgow, Thursday, 16th September 2010

Dear Brothers and Sisters in Christ,

"The Kingdom of God is very near to you!" *(Lk 10:9)*. With these words of the Gospel we have just heard, I greet all of you with great affection in the Lord. Truly the Lord's Kingdom is already in our midst! At this Eucharistic celebration in which the Church in

Scotland gathers around the altar in union with the Successor of Peter, let us reaffirm our faith in Christ's word and our hope – a hope which never disappoints – in his promises! I warmly greet Cardinal O'Brien and the Scottish bishops; I thank in particular Archbishop Conti for his kind words of welcome on your behalf;

and I express my deep gratitude for the work that the British and Scottish Governments and the Glasgow city fathers have done to make this occasion possible.

Today's Gospel reminds us that Christ continues to send his disciples into the world in order to proclaim the coming of his Kingdom and to bring his peace   >

into the world, beginning house by house, family by family, town by town. I have come as a herald of that peace to you, the spiritual children of St Andrew and to confirm you in the faith of Peter *(cf.Lk 22:32)*. It is with some emotion that I address you, not far from the spot where my beloved predecessor Pope John Paul II celebrated Mass nearly 30 years ago with you and was welcomed by the largest crowd ever gathered in Scottish history.

Much has happened in Scotland and in the Church in this country since that historic visit. I note with great satisfaction how Pope John Paul's call to you to walk hand in hand with your fellow Christians has led to greater trust and friendship with the members of the Church of Scotland, the Scottish

Episcopal Church and others. Let me encourage you to continue to pray and work with them in building a brighter future for Scotland based upon our common Christian heritage. In today's first reading we heard St Paul appeal to the Romans to acknowledge that, as members of Christ's body, we belong to each other *(cf. Rom 12:5)* and to live in respect and mutual love. In that spirit I greet the ecumenical representatives who honour us by their presence. This year marks the 450th anniversary of the Reformation Parliament, but also the 100th anniversary of the World Missionary Conference in Edinburgh, which is widely acknowledged to mark the birth of the modern ecumenical movement. Let us give thanks to God for the promise which

St Ninian, whose feast we celebrate today, was himself unafraid to be a lone voice. In the footsteps of the disciples whom Our Lord sent forth before him, Ninian was one of the very first Catholic missionaries to bring his fellow Britons the good news of Jesus Christ. His mission church in Galloway became a centre for the first evangelisation of this country.

(above) © Osiowy/www.thepapalvisit.org.uk
(right) © Mazur/www.thepapalvisit.org.uk

ecumenical understanding and co-operation represents for a united witness to the saving truth of God's word in today's rapidly changing society.

Among the differing gifts which St Paul lists for the building up of the Church is that of teaching *(cf. Rom 12:7)*. The preaching of the Gospel has always been accompanied by concern for the word: the inspired word of God and the culture in which that word takes root and flourishes. Here in Scotland, I think of the three medieval universities founded here by the popes, including that of St Andrews' which is beginning to mark the 600th anniversary of its foundation. In the last 30 years and with the assistance of civil authorities, Scottish Catholic schools have taken up the challenge of providing an integral education to greater numbers of students, and this has helped young people not only along the path of spiritual and human growth, but also in entering the professions and public life. This is a sign of great hope for the Church, and I encourage the Catholic professionals, politicians and >

1. A nun waves a papal flag after Pope Benedict XVI celebrated Mass at Bellahouston Park in Glasgow. © Catholic News Service.

2. Anton McManus, who was diagnosed with cancer, with the letter he wrote to the Pope asking him to "help keep his cancer away". © PA Photos.

3. Anton receiving a blessing by the pontiff after celebrating Mass at Bellahouston Park.
© Mazur/www.papalvisit.org.uk

teachers of Scotland never to lose sight of their calling to use their talents and experience in the service of the faith, engaging contemporary Scottish culture at every level.

The evangelisation of culture is all the more important in our times, when a "dictatorship of relativism" threatens to obscure the unchanging truth about man's nature, his destiny and his ultimate good. There are some who now seek to exclude religious belief from public discourse, to privatise it or even to paint it as a threat to equality and liberty. Yet religion is in fact a guarantee of authentic liberty and respect, leading us to look upon every person as a brother or sister. For this reason I appeal in particular to you, the lay faithful, in accordance with your baptismal calling and mission, not only to be examples of faith in public, but also to put the case for the promotion of faith's wisdom and vision in the public forum. Society today needs clear voices which propose our right to live, not in a jungle of self-destructive and arbitrary freedoms, but in a society which works for the true welfare of its citizens and offers them guidance and protection in the face of their weakness and fragility. Do not be afraid to take up this service to your brothers and sisters, and to the future of your beloved nation.

St Ninian, whose feast we celebrate today, was himself unafraid to be a lone voice. In the footsteps of the disciples whom Our Lord sent forth before him, Ninian was one of the very first Catholic missionaries to bring his fellow Britons the good news of Jesus Christ. His mission church in Galloway became a centre for the first evangelisation of this country. That work was later taken up by St Mungo, Glasgow's own patron, and by other saints, the greatest of who must include St Columba and St Margaret. Inspired by them, many men and women have laboured over many centuries to hand down the faith to you. Strive to be worthy of this great tradition! Let the exhortation of St Paul in the first reading be your constant inspiration: "Do not lag in zeal, be ardent in spirit, serve the Lord. Rejoice in hope, be patient in suffering and persevere in prayer" (cf. Rom 12:11-12).

I would now like to address a special word to the bishops of Scotland. Dear brothers, let me encourage you in your pastoral leadership of the Catholics of Scotland. As you know, one of your first pastoral duties is to your priests (cf. Presbyterorum Ordinis, 7) and to their sanctification. As they are alter Christus to the Catholic community, so you are to them. Live to the full the charity that flows from Christ, in your brotherly ministry towards your priests, collaborating with them all, and in particular with those who have little contact with their fellow priests. Pray with them for vocations, that the Lord of the harvest will send labourers to his harvest (cf. Lk 10:2).

Just as the Eucharist makes the Church, so the priesthood is central to the life of the Church. Engage yourselves personally in forming your priests as a body of men who inspire others to dedicate themselves completely to the service of Almighty God. Have a care also for your deacons, whose ministry of service is associated in a particular way with that of the order of bishops. Be a father and a guide in holiness for them, encouraging them to grow in knowledge and wisdom in carrying out the mission of herald to which they have been called.

Dear priests of Scotland, you are called to holiness and to serve God's people by modeling your lives on the mystery of the Lord's cross. Preach the Gospel with a pure heart and a clear conscience. Dedicate yourselves to God alone and you will become shining examples to young men of a holy, simple and joyful life: they, in their turn, will surely wish to join you in your single-minded service of God's people. May the example of St John Ogilvie, dedicated, selfless and brave, inspire all of you. Similarly, let me encourage you, the monks, nuns and religious of Scotland to be a light on a hilltop, living an authentic Christian life of prayer and action that witnesses in a luminous way to the power of the Gospel.

Finally, I would like to say a word to you, my dear young Catholics of Scotland. I urge you to lead lives worthy of Our Lord (cf. Eph 4:1) and of yourselves. There are many temptations placed before you every day - drugs, money, sex, pornography, alcohol - which the world tells you will bring you happiness, yet these things are destructive and divisive. There is only one thing which lasts: the love of Jesus Christ personally for each one of you. Search for him, know him and love him, and he will set you free

from slavery to the glittering but superficial existence frequently proposed by today's society. Put aside what is worthless and learn of your own dignity as children of God. In today's Gospel, Jesus asks us to pray for vocations: I pray that many of you will know and love Jesus Christ and, through that encounter, will dedicate yourselves completely to God, especially those of you who are called to the priesthood and religious life. This is the challenge the Lord gives to you today: the Church now belongs to you!

Dear friends, I express once more my joy at celebrating this Mass with you. I am happy to assure you of my prayers in the ancient language of your country: **Sìth agus beannachd Dhe dhuibh uile; Dia bhi timcheall oirbh; agus gum beannaicheadh Dia Alba. God's peace and blessing to you all; God surround you; and may God bless the people of Scotland!** ∎

A pilgrim's message

When I left Bellahouston the very happy crowds were slowly wending their way back to various stations and to their coaches, which had been parked on the (closed) M77. There was a wonderful spirit in the air, as pilgrims called out their thanks to the police who were everywhere. The mounted police were allowing children to stroke their horses. Those horses must have been as tired as we were, but they remained calm and still. We were shepherded to Dumbreck station and formed an orderly queue for the train back to Edinburgh Central. I fell into conversation with a group of ladies and asked them how the day had been for them. They were thrilled, and said it had been magical. One of them had been privileged to be a minister of Holy Communion and told me about how the youngsters with the yellow umbrellas had looked after her. It was just one of many incidents that day when young and old were united in joy and praise.

I asked them which of the songs had been their favourite and was surprised, a little, to learn that it was the *Pater Noster*. I suspect that each group of pilgrims would have a different choice, and one of the great things about the planning of this Mass was the wide range of musical styles, making sure there was something for everyone. The ladies were also very impressed at the quietness of the crowd just before Mass started. People were easily able to move from the cheering, banner-waving exuberance to prayerful expectancy and reverence.

On the train from Glasgow Queen Street to Edinburgh, I found myself sitting next to a BBC cameraman, who had been working on a programme for the World Service, to be broadcast in Arabic for the Maronite community. This man, who was a veteran of the last papal visit, told me he thought the crowd today had been a good deal larger than forecast. He used a curious way to estimate the size of the crowd, by comparing it with a maximum capacity Manchester United crowd. Using this measure, he estimated the crowd as 75,000. After so much gloomy talk of 'unsold tickets' it seems that the prophets of doom were wrong. ■   http://thepapalvisit.wordpress.com/

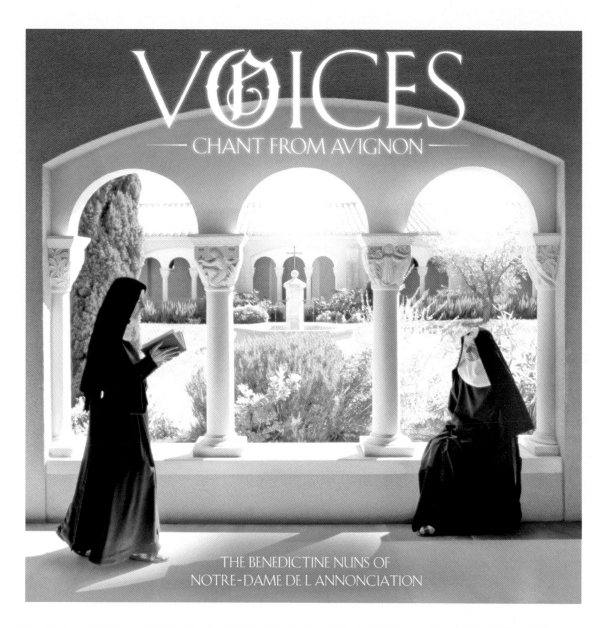

> "THE MOST IMPORTANT THING IN PRAYER AND SONG IS FOR US TO FOCUS ON THE FACT THAT WE ARE SINGING FOR GOD"
> (Mother Abbess)

Voices – Chant From Avignon is an album of beautiful, soothing Gregorian chant, recorded by the Benedictine Nuns of Notre-Dame de l'Annonciation in their Abbey near Avignon in Southern France.

The Nuns were 'discovered' after an extensive world-wide search for the best choral ensemble, and have created an album of evocative tranquility and inner-purity.

This extraordinary album is released on November 8th 2010 but can be pre-ordered now via Amazon.

The community has granted unprecedented access to their cloistered way of life through a series of films and interviews. To see these and hear preview tracks from the album, go to www.chantfromavignon.com

www.chantfromavignon.com

The Pope arrived a little late at St Mary's University College, Twickenham, but he paused to greet some of the uniformed young students one by one, shaking their hands and accepting bouquets.

In a sense, Pope Benedict, a former university professor, was back in his favourite milieu. But on this particular day, he was to speak more as a pastor than a theologian, offering a straightforward lesson on the path of sainthood.

Speech welcoming Pope Benedict to the 'Big Assembly'

St Mary's University College, Twickenham, Friday 17th September 2010

Pope Benedict,

It is my honour to welcome you to this celebration of Catholic Education in England, Scotland and Wales. You can see for yourself what great joy your visit brings to our hearts. Today, we celebrate the many generations of young people who were educated in Catholic schools and colleges and have subsequently taken their place in society to serve the common good.

Bishop Malcolm McMahon introduces Pope Benedict XVI to 'The Big Assembly' gathering at St Mary's University College Twickenham. © PA Photos.

We celebrate the wonderful sense of faith and community that characterises our schools. And we celebrate with you, our faith, our love, and our hope for the future.

At the heart of Catholic education is our understanding that young people shall have life and have it to the full. That is our theme today. Christ's words guide us as we strive to educate our children, because we believe that true fulfilment of the human person can only come through a close friendship with Christ. All that happens in Catholic education is based on our belief that a human person is made in the image of God and this is most fully expressed in the desire to know and to love.By educating children and expanding each one's capacity for love, we develop the whole person, nurturing body, spirit and mind alike. Today one in ten young people is educated at one of England's 2,200 Catholic schools, with many more in Scotland and Wales. Thousands more young and mature students receive further and higher education in our colleges.

Holy Father, this Big Assembly celebrates some of the powerful forces which connect the students, schools and colleges, and help people live life to the full: Community, friendship, sport and of course faith. Such fulfilled lives are only made possible through the relationship between State and Church. Our unique relationship with our government, which we value very much, has enabled Catholic schools and University Colleges to make an enormous contribution to the life of our society.

We are also assisted by many members of staff and governors who are not Catholics, but who subscribe to the ethos of Catholic education. In your presence, Holy Father, I thank them on behalf of the Catholic community. Our schools and colleges are also integrated into parish communities, local authorities and school networks. A sense of these connections can be felt today with so many children from so many schools and boroughs coming together to greet you, Holy Father, at this Big Assembly.

They are far from alone, through the internet and television, this event is being attended by young people, their families and parish communities, throughout the world - coming together to celebrate this occasion with you. Each will remember this day for years to come. And you can be assured, Holy Father, that they will remember you in their prayers as you continue your visit to the United Kingdom. And finally, I want to announce that following your historic visit in England and Wales, we'll be celebrating a year of Catholic education, and this will recognise past achievements, but also look forward to a future where we ensure that only the best education is delivered to our young people.

**Holy Father, welcome to 'The Big Assembly'.
The Rt Rev Malcolm McMahon
Bishop of Nottingham. ■**

Pope Benedict addresses Teachers and Religious

Chapel of St Mary's University College, Twickenham, Friday 17th September 2010. 11:30am

Your Excellency the Secretary of State for Education, Bishop Stack, Dr. Naylor, Reverend Fathers, Brothers and Sisters in Christ,

I am pleased to have this opportunity to pay tribute to the outstanding contribution made by religious men and women in this land to the noble task of education. I thank the young people for their fine singing, and I thank Sr. Teresa for her words. To her and to all the dedicated men and women who devote their lives to teaching the young, I want to express sentiments of deep appreciation. You form new generations not only in knowledge of the faith, but in every aspect of what it means to live as mature and responsible citizens in today's world.

As you know, the task of a teacher is not simply to impart information or to provide training in skills intended to deliver some economic benefit to society; education is not and must never be considered as purely utilitarian. It is about forming the human person, equipping him or her to live life to the full – in short it is about imparting wisdom. And true wisdom is inseparable from knowledge of the Creator, for "both we and our words are in his hand, as are all understanding and skill in crafts" (Wis 7:16). This transcendent dimension of study >

and teaching was clearly grasped by the monks who contributed so much to the evangelisation of these islands. I am thinking of the Benedictines who accompanied St Augustine on his mission to England, of the disciples of St Columba who spread the faith across Scotland and Northern England, of St David and his companions in Wales. Since the search for God, which lies at the heart of the monastic vocation, requires active engagement with the means by which he makes himself known – his creation and his revealed word – it was only natural that the monastery should have a library and a school *(cf. Address to representatives from the world of culture at the "Collège des Bernardins" in Paris, 12th September 2008).* It was the monks' dedication to learning as the path on which to encounter the Incarnate Word of God that was to lay the foundations of our Western culture and civilisation.

Looking around me today, I see many apostolic religious whose charism includes the education of the young. This gives me an opportunity to give thanks to God for the life and work of the Venerable Mary Ward, a native of this land whose pioneering vision of apostolic religious life for women has borne so much fruit. I myself as a young boy was taught by the 'English Ladies' and I owe them a deep debt of gratitude. Many of you belong to teaching orders that have carried the light of the Gospel to far-off lands as

(above) Pope Benedict XVI begins a service in the chapel at St Mary's University College in Twickenham.
© Charlotte Bromley Davenport
//www.thepapalvisit.org.uk

part of the Church's great missionary work, and for this too I give thanks and praise to God. Often you laid the foundations of educational provision long before the State assumed a responsibility for this vital service to the individual and to society. As the relative roles of Church and State in the field of education continue to evolve, never forget that religious have a unique contribution to offer to this apostolate, above all through lives consecrated to God and through faithful, loving witness to Christ, the supreme Teacher.

Indeed, the presence of religious in Catholic schools is a powerful reminder of the much-discussed Catholic ethos that needs to inform every aspect of school life. This extends far beyond the self-evident requirement that the content of the teaching should always be in conformity with Church doctrine. It means that the life of faith needs to be the driving force behind every activity in the school, so that the Church's mission may be served effectively, and the young people may discover the joy of entering into Christ's "being for others" *(Spe Salvi, 28)*.

Before I conclude, I wish to add a particular word of appreciation for those whose task it is to ensure that our schools provide a safe environment for children and young people. Our responsibility towards those entrusted to us for their Christian formation demands nothing less. Indeed, the life of faith can only be effectively nurtured when the prevailing atmosphere is one of respectful and affectionate trust. I pray that this may continue to be a hallmark of the Catholic schools in this country.

With these sentiments, dear Brothers and Sisters, I invite you now to stand and pray. ■

A Headteacher's view

A brief account from the Headteacher of a Richmond Primary School.

© Mazur/www.thepapalvisit.org.uk

Met my four children at 7.20 this morning and eventually got into St Mary's College around 9.45. The security was amazing, the streets were lined with police and we had to go through an airport style security system to get on the site. I nearly did not get in as I was wearing a dress and jacket with jet beads set in metal and kept setting off the alarm. Short of taking off my dress I was not sure how I was going to get in! Finally they decided I was not a rampant terrorist but a mundane Headteacher and let me through. My children and I were part of the welcoming group of about 350 people who stood outside the chapel. We were only about 10ft away from the Pope both when he got out of the car he travelled from Wimbledon in and when he got in the popemobile. He actually shook hands with many of the Richmond children and even picked up one of the children and kissed his head which was lovely but sadly not one of mine! We then went onto the college field to watch 'The Big Assembly' which was great. On his way out of the arena the Pope again came very close to us! Quite a special day! ■ http://thepapalvisit.wordpress.com/

Pope Benedict's address to pupils

Sports Arena of St Mary's University College, Twickenham,
Friday, 17th September 2010. 11:45am

Dear Brothers and Sisters in Christ,
Dear young friends,
First of all, I want to say how glad I am to be here with you today. I greet you most warmly, those who have come to St Mary's University from Catholic schools and colleges across the United Kingdom, and all who are watching on television and via the internet. I thank Bishop McMahon for his gracious

welcome, I thank the choir and the band for the lovely music which began our celebration, and I thank Miss Bellot for her kind words on behalf of all the young people present. In view of London's forthcoming Olympic Games, it has been a pleasure to inaugurate this Sports Foundation, named in honour of Pope John Paul II, and I pray that all who come here will give glory to God

(opposite) People look on as Pope Benedict XVI attends 'The Big Assembly' a celebration of Catholic education at St Mary's University College, Twickenham.

(above right) Pope Benedict XVI wearing a blue batik stole sent by students watching via internet in Gambia. © PA Photos.

through their sporting activities, as well as bringing enjoyment to themselves and to others.

It is not often that a Pope, or indeed anyone else, has the opportunity to speak to the students of all the Catholic schools of England, Wales and Scotland at the same time. And since I have the chance now, there is something I very much want to say to you. I hope that among those of you listening to me today there are some of the future saints of the 21st century. What God wants most of all for each one of you is that you should become holy. He loves you much more than you could ever begin to imagine, and he wants the very best for you. And by far the best thing for you is to grow in holiness.

Perhaps some of you have never thought about this before. Perhaps some of you think being a saint is not for you. Let me explain what I mean. When we are young, we can usually think of people that we look up to, people we admire, people we want to be like. It could be someone we meet >

Manchester City Assistant Manager Brian Kidd (left) lights a candle during 'The Big Assembly', a celebration of Catholic education, at St Mary's University College, Twickenham. © PA Photos.

in our daily lives that we hold in great esteem. Or it could be someone famous. We live in a celebrity culture, and young people are often encouraged to model themselves on figures from the world of sport or entertainment. My question for you is this: what are the qualities you see in others that you would most like to have yourselves? What kind of person would you really like to be?

When I invite you to become saints, I am asking you not to be content with second best. I am asking you not to pursue one limited goal and ignore all the others. Having money makes it possible to be generous and to do good in the world, but on its own, it is not enough to make us happy. Being highly skilled in some activity or profession is good, but it will not satisfy us unless we aim for something greater still. It might make us famous, but it will not make us happy. Happiness is something we all want, but one of the great tragedies in this world is that so many people never find it, because they look for it in the wrong places. The key to it is very simple – true happiness is to be found in God. We need to have the courage to place our deepest hopes in God alone, not in money, in a career, in worldly success, or in our relationships with others, but in God. Only he can satisfy the deepest needs of our hearts.

Not only does God love us with a depth and an intensity that we can scarcely begin to comprehend, but he invites us to respond to that love. You all know what it is like when you meet someone interesting and attractive, and you want to be that person's friend. You always hope they will find you interesting and attractive, and want to be your friend. God wants your friendship. And once you enter into friendship with God, everything in your life begins to change. As you come to know him better, you find you want to reflect something of his infinite goodness in your own life. You are attracted to the practice of virtue. You begin to see greed and selfishness and all the other sins for what they really are, destructive and dangerous tendencies that cause deep suffering and do great damage, and you want to avoid falling into that trap yourselves. You begin to feel compassion for people in difficulties and you are eager to do something to help them. You want to come to the aid of the poor and the hungry, you want to comfort the sorrowful, you want to be kind and generous. And once these >

The students presented the Pope with three books to add to his own library: a volume written by St Bede, a book of Scottish poetry and a book about the Catholic martyrs of Wales.

Just one new priest can make all the difference

With the generous help of supporters, the **Society of St Peter the Apostle (SPA)** funds the training of EVERY seminarian in ALL Catholic mission dioceses.

We need your help to make sure seminaries stay open, vocations are not turned away and new priests are trained to bring the light of faith and hope to their communities.

Please consider sharing your faith with future generations by including the SPA in your Will.

In gratitude, Mass is offered daily at St Peter's Basilica, Rome, for all SPA benefactors, living and deceased.

To request an information leaflet about how to leave a gift to the SPA (with no obligation) or to make a donation please contact:

Mgr John Dale, National Director, SPA, 23 Eccleston Square, London SW1V 1NU Telephone 020 7821 9755

Missio is part of the Pontifical Mission Societies worldwide network Reg. Charity No. 1056651 Email:spa@missio.org.uk

Web: www.missio.org.uk

SPAUNS/910

things begin to matter to you, you are well on the way to becoming saints.

In your Catholic schools, there is always a bigger picture over and above the individual subjects you study, the different skills you learn. All the work you do is placed in the context of growing in friendship with God, and all that flows from that friendship. So you learn not just to be good students, but good citizens, good people. As you move higher up the school, you have to make choices regarding the subjects you study, you begin to specialise with a view to what you are going to do later on in life. That is right and proper. But always remember that every subject you study is part of a bigger picture. Never allow yourselves to become narrow. The world needs good scientists, but a scientific outlook becomes dangerously narrow if it ignores the religious or ethical dimension of life, just as religion becomes narrow if it rejects the legitimate contribution of science to our understanding of the world. We need good historians and philosophers and economists, but if the account they give of human life within their particular field is too narrowly focused, they can lead us seriously astray.

A good school provides a rounded education for the whole person. And a good Catholic school, over and above this, should help all its students to become saints. I know that there are many non-Catholics studying in the Catholic schools in Great Britain, and I wish to include all of you in my words today. I pray that you too will feel encouraged to practise virtue and to grow in knowledge and friendship with God alongside your Catholic classmates. You are a reminder to them of the bigger picture that exists outside the school, and indeed, it is only right that respect and friendship for members of other religious traditions should be among the virtues learned in a Catholic school. I hope too that you will want to share with everyone you meet the values and insights you have learned through the Christian education you have received.

Dear friends, I thank you for your attention, I promise to pray for you, and I ask you to pray for me. I hope to see many of you next August, at the World Youth Day in Madrid. In the meantime, may God bless you all! ∎

(above) A child looks on as Pope Benedict XVI attends 'The Big Assembly', a celebration of Catholic education at St Mary's University College, Twickenham. © PA Photos.

Archbishop Kelly welcomes the Pope to the Interreligious Gathering

Waldegrave Drawing Room, St Mary's University College, Twickenham, Friday 17th September 2010. 12:30pm

Most Holy Father,

When I remember him, I find I give ever greater thanks to God for your predecessor, Paul VI, who referred to this land as a 'terreno ecumenico' - ecumenical land.

The story of this land, including the fact that blood was once shed because of conflicts about the way of life Christ, offers specific challenges and opportunities in the ecumenical journey to which the Holy Spirit calls us in our day. To that journey, in all its complexity, you are devoting time in this coming part of this day.

But it seems to me because of our complex history, again with dark days and indeed blood shed through issues of domination, culture, race and religion, I feel this is a unique terrain in an aspect of life across today's world, which gathers us all here today.

There are specific challenges and opportunities which we have had to face and still face, if we would discern together how to be always and everywhere instruments of justice and peace.

We thank you, and I do so in great confidence in the light of the sharing that's taken place here this morning. We thank you for your presence and your words. And we promise that we'll be faithful to the way of truth, wisdom, holiness and peace. ■

Pope Benedict's Speech to Representatives of other Religions

Waldegrave Drawing Room, St Mary's University College, Twickenham, Friday 17th September 2010. 12:45pm

Distinguished guests, dear friends,

I am very pleased to have this opportunity to meet you, the representatives of the various religious communities in Great Britain. I greet both the ministers of religion present and those of you who are active in politics, business and industry. I am grateful to Dr. Azzam and to Chief Rabbi Lord Sacks for the greetings which they have expressed on your behalf. As I salute you, let me also wish the Jewish community in Britain and throughout the world a happy and holy celebration of Yom Kippur.

I would like to begin my remarks by expressing the Catholic Church's appreciation for the important witness that all of you bear as spiritual men and women living at a time when religious convictions are not always understood or appreciated. The presence of committed believers in various fields of social and economic life speaks eloquently of the fact that the spiritual dimension of our lives is fundamental to our identity as human beings, that man, in other words, does not live by bread alone (cf. Deut 8:3). As followers of different religious traditions working together for the good of the community at large, we attach great importance to this 'side by side' dimension of our cooperation, which complements the 'face to face' aspect of our continuing dialogue.

On the spiritual level, all of us, in our different ways, are personally engaged in a journey that grants an answer to the most important question of all – the question concerning the ultimate meaning of our human existence. The quest for the sacred is the search for the one thing necessary, which alone satisfies the longings of the human heart. In the fifth century, St Augustine described that search in these terms: "Lord, you have created us for yourself and our hearts are restless until they rest in you" (Confessions, Book I, 1). As we embark on this adventure we come to realise more and more that the initiative lies not with us, but with the Lord: it is not so much we who are seeking him, but rather he >

who is seeking us, indeed it was he who placed that longing for him deep within our hearts.

Your presence and witness in the world points towards the fundamental importance for human life of this spiritual quest in which we are engaged. Within their own spheres of competence, the human and natural sciences provide us with an invaluable understanding of aspects of our existence and they deepen our grasp of the workings of the physical universe, which can then be harnessed in order to bring great benefit to the human family. Yet these disciplines do not and cannot answer the fundamental question, because they operate on another level altogether. They cannot satisfy the deepest longings of the human heart, they cannot fully explain to us our origin and our destiny, why and for what purpose we exist, nor indeed can they provide us with an exhaustive answer to the question, "Why is there something rather than nothing?"

The quest for the sacred does not devalue other fields of human enquiry. On the contrary, it places them in a context which magnifies their importance, as ways of responsibly exercising our stewardship over creation. In the Bible, we read that, after the work of creation was completed, God blessed our first parents and said to them, "Be fruitful and multiply, and fill the earth and subdue it" *(Gen 1:28)*. He entrusted us with the task of exploring and harnessing the mysteries of nature in order to serve a higher good. What is that higher good? In the Christian faith, it is expressed as love for God and love for our neighbour. And so we engage with the world wholeheartedly and enthusiastically, but always with a view to serving that higher good, lest we disfigure the beauty of creation by exploiting it for selfish purposes.

So it is that genuine religious belief points us beyond present utility towards the transcendent. It reminds us of the possibility and the imperative of moral conversion, of the duty to live peaceably with our

1. Pope Benedict XVI speaks at a meeting of religious leaders at St Mary's University College Chapel in Twickenham. © PA Photos.

2. Pope Benedict XVI meets Britain's Chief Rabbi Jonathan Sacks. © PA Photos.

3. Pope Benedict XVI with Britain's Baroness Warsi. © Catholic News Service.

neighbour, of the importance of living a life of integrity. Properly understood, it brings enlightenment, it purifies our hearts and it inspires noble and generous action, to the benefit of the entire human family. It motivates us to cultivate the practice of virtue and to reach out towards one another in love, with the greatest respect for religious traditions different from our own.

Ever since the Second Vatican Council, the Catholic Church has placed special emphasis on the importance of dialogue and co-operation with the followers of other religions. In order to be fruitful, this requires reciprocity on the part of all partners in dialogue and the followers of other religions. I am thinking in particular of situations in some parts of the world, where co-operation and dialogue between religions calls for mutual respect, the freedom to practise one's religion and to engage in acts of public worship, and the freedom to follow one's conscience without suffering ostracism or persecution, even after conversion from one religion to another. Once such a respect and openness has been established, peoples of all religions will work together effectively for peace and mutual understanding, and so give a convincing witness before the world.

This kind of dialogue needs to take place on a number of different levels, and should not be limited to formal discussions. The dialogue of life involves simply living alongside one another and learning from one another in such a way as to grow in mutual knowledge and respect. The dialogue of action brings us together in concrete forms of collaboration, as we apply our religious insights to the task of promoting integral human development, working for peace, justice and the stewardship of creation. Such a dialogue may include exploring together how to defend human life at every stage and how to ensure the non-exclusion of the religious dimension of individuals and communities in the life of society. Then at the level of formal conversations, there is a need not only for theological exchange, but also sharing our spiritual riches, speaking of our experience of prayer and contemplation, and expressing to one another the joy of our encounter with divine love. In this context I am pleased to note the many positive initiatives undertaken in this country to promote such dialogue at a variety of levels. As the Catholic Bishops of England and Wales noted in their

recent document *Meeting God in Friend and Stranger,* the effort to reach out in friendship to followers of other religions is becoming a familiar part of the mission of the local Church *(n. 228)*, a characteristic feature of the religious landscape in this country.

My dear friends, as I conclude my remarks, let me assure you that the Catholic Church follows the path of engagement and dialogue out of a genuine sense of respect for you and your beliefs. Catholics, both in Britain and throughout the world, will continue to work to build bridges of friendship to other religions, to heal past wrongs and to foster trust between individuals and communities. Let me reiterate my thanks for your welcome and my gratitude for this opportunity to offer you my encouragement for your dialogue with your Christian sisters and brothers. Upon all of you I invoke abundant divine blessings! Thank you very much. ■

Archbishop of Canterbury's Speech to Pope Benedict

Lambeth Palace, Friday 17th September 2010 . 4:30pm

Your Holiness, brother bishops, brothers and sisters in Christ:
It is a particular pleasure that on this historic occasion we are able to come together as bishops of the Roman Catholic and Anglican churches in this country to greet you, Your Holiness, during a visit which we all hope will be of significance both to the Church of Christ and to British society. Your consistent and penetrating analysis of the state of European society in general has been a major contribution to public debate on the relations between Church and culture, and we gratefully acknowledge our debt in this respect.

Our task as bishops is to preach the Gospel and shepherd the flock of Christ; and this includes the responsibility not only to feed but also to protect it from harm. Today, this involves a readiness to respond to the various trends in our cultural environment that seek to present Christian faith as both an obstacle to human freedom and a scandal to human intellect. We need to be clear that the Gospel of the new creation in Jesus Christ is the door through which we enter into true liberty and true understanding: we are made free to be human as God intends us to be human; we are given the illumination that helps us see one another and all created things in the light of divine love and intelligence. As you said in your Inaugural Mass in 2005, recalling your predecessor's first words as pope, Christ takes away nothing "that pertains to human freedom or dignity or to the building of a just society… If we let Christ into our lives we lose absolutely nothing of what makes life free, beautiful and great. Only in his friendship is the great potential of human existence revealed."
[Inaugural Homily, Rome, 24 April 2005]

Our presence together as British bishops here today is a sign of the way in which, in this country, we see our task as one and indivisible. The International Anglican-Roman Catholic Commission on Unity and Mission has set before us all the vital importance of our common calling as bishops to be agents of mission. Our fervent prayer is that this visit will give us fresh energy and vision for working together in this context in the name of what a great Roman Catholic thinker of the last century called 'true humanism' – a passionate commitment to the dignity of all human beings, from the beginning to the end of life, and to a resistance to every tyranny that threatens to stifle or deny the place of the transcendent in human affairs.

We do not as churches seek political power or control, or the dominance of Christian faith in the public sphere; but the opportunity to testify, to argue, sometimes to protest, sometimes to affirm – to play our part in the public debates of our societies. And we shall, of course, be effective not when we have mustered enough political leverage to get our way but when we have persuaded our neighbours that the life of faith is a life well lived and joyfully lived.

In other words, we shall be effective defenders or proclaimers of our faith when we can show what a holy life looks like, a life in which the joy of God is transparently present. And this means that our ministry together as bishops across the still-surviving boundaries of our confessions is not only a search for how we best act together in the public arena; it is a quest together for holiness and transparency to God, a search for ways in which we may help each other to grow in the life of the Holy Spirit. As you have said, Your Holiness, "a joint fundamental testimony of faith ought to be given before a world which is torn by doubts and shaken by fears." *['Luther* >

Pope Benedict XVI is greeted by the Archbishop of Canterbury Dr. Rowan Williams, as he arrives at Lambeth Palace on the second day of his State Visit. © PA Photos.

and the Unity of the Churches', 1983]

In 1845, when John Henry Newman finally decided that he must follow his conscience and seek his future in serving God in communion with the See of Rome, one of his most intimate Anglican friends and allies, the priest Edward Bouverie Pusey, whose memory the Church of England marked in its liturgical calendar yesterday, wrote a moving meditation on this 'parting of friends' in which he said of the separation between Anglicans and Roman Catholics: "it is what is unholy on both sides that keeps us apart".

That should not surprise us: holiness is at its simplest fellowship with Christ; and when that fellowship with Christ is brought to maturity, so is our fellowship with one another. As bishops, we are servants of the unity of Christ's people, Christ's one Body. And, meeting as we do as bishops of separated church communities, we must all feel that each of our own ministries is made less by the fact of our dividedness, a very real but imperfect communion. Perhaps we shall not quickly overcome the remaining obstacles to full, restored communion; but no obstacles stand in the way of our seeking, as a matter of joyful obedience to the Lord, more ways in which to build up one another in holiness by prayer and public celebration together, by closer friendship, and by growing together both in the challenging work of service for all whom Christ loves, and mission to all God has made.

May this historic visit be for all of us a special time of grace and of growth in our shared calling, as you, Your Holiness, bring us the word of the Gospel afresh. ∎

© **Rowan Williams 2010**

Pope Benedict's address to the Archbishop of Canterbury

Lambeth Palace, Friday 17th September 2010 . 4:30pm

Your Grace,

It is a pleasure for me to be able to return the courtesy of the visits you have made to me in Rome by a fraternal visit to you here in your official residence. I thank you for your invitation and for the hospitality that you have so generously provided. I greet too the Anglican bishops gathered here from different parts of the United Kingdom, my brother bishops from the Catholic Dioceses of England, Wales and Scotland, and the ecumenical advisers who are present.

You have spoken, Your Grace, of the historic meeting that took place, almost 30 years ago, between two of our predecessors – Pope John Paul II and Archbishop Robert Runcie – in Canterbury Cathedral. There, in the very place where St Thomas of Canterbury bore witness to Christ by the shedding of his blood, they prayed together for the gift of unity among the followers of Christ. We continue today to pray for that gift, knowing that the unity Christ willed for his disciples will only come about in answer to prayer, through the action of the Holy Spirit, who ceaselessly renews the Church and guides her into the fullness of truth.

It is not my intention today to speak of the difficulties that the ecumenical path has encountered and continues to encounter. Those difficulties are well known to everyone here. Rather, I wish to join you in giving thanks for the deep friendship that has grown between us and for the remarkable progress that has been made in so many areas of dialogue during the 40 years that have elapsed since the Anglican-Roman Catholic International Commission began its work. Let us entrust the fruits of that work to the Lord of the harvest, confident that he will bless our friendship with further significant growth.

The context in which dialogue takes place between the Anglican Communion and the Catholic Church has evolved in dramatic ways since the private meeting between Pope John XXIII and Archbishop Geoffrey Fisher in 1960. On the one hand, the surrounding culture is growing ever more distant from its Christian roots, despite a deep and widespread hunger for spiritual nourishment. On the other hand, the increasingly multicultural dimension of society, particularly marked in this country, brings with it the opportunity to encounter other religions. For us Christians this opens up the possibility of exploring, together with members of other religious traditions, ways of bearing witness to the transcendent dimension of the human person and the universal call to holiness, leading to the practice of virtue in our personal and social lives. Ecumenical co-operation in this task remains essential, and will surely bear fruit in promoting peace and harmony in a world that so often seems at risk of fragmentation.

At the same time, we Christians >

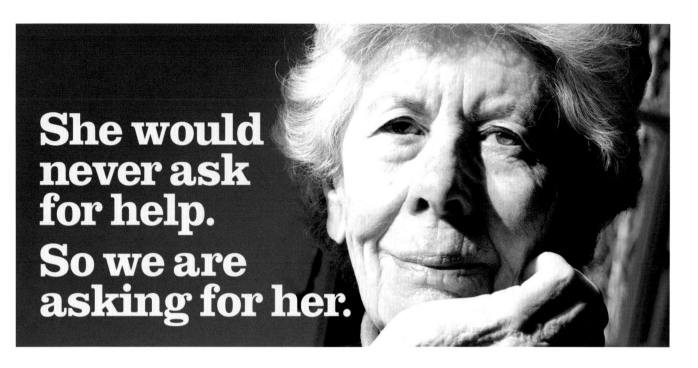

She would never ask for help. So we are asking for her.

Mary is typical of the sort of person who has worked hard all her life and never needed to ask for help. She has dedicated her life to helping others through her work as a nurse.

Unfortunately, earlier this year Mary's husband died and she had to use her savings to pay for his funeral. She then became ill and had to give up work. It wasn't long before Mary found she was struggling to afford food and heating. Luckily a friend of Mary's had heard about our charity, Elizabeth Finn Care, and she managed to persuade her to contact us for help. We now provide Mary with regular funding.

Elizabeth Finn Care is a direct grant-giving charity dedicated specifically to helping those living in

financial need. Elizabeth Finn Care also provides information on welfare benefits and charitable grants through the Turn2us website service www.turn2us.org.uk

In order to continue helping people like Mary and the large number of people who are living below the poverty line in this country, we rely on people such as yourself to make a donation. If you would be interested in leaving a legacy to Elizabeth Finn Care in your Will, or making a donation to the charity, please contact us using the details below.

Call: 020 8834 9261
Email: legacyinfo@elizabethfinn.org.uk
Or send for your free guide below.

✂ - ✂

Please send to: Elizabeth Finn Care, Hythe House, 200 Shepherds Bush Road, London, W6 7NL

Title:	First Name:	Surname:

Address:

| | Postcode: |

Telephone:

  REMEMBER US IN YOUR WILL Help our work live on...

www.elizabethfinncare.org.uk A charity registered in England and Wales: 207812 and Scotland: SC040987. www.turn2us.org.uk Turn2us is part of Elizabeth Finn Care.
Ref: PVis1010

Pope Benedict XVI addresses a meeting of Anglican and Roman Catholic diocesan bishops of England, Scotland and Wales, flanked by the Archbishop of Canterbury Dr. Rowan Williams at Lambeth Palace in London. © PA Photos.

must never hesitate to proclaim our faith in the uniqueness of the salvation won for us by Christ, and to explore together a deeper understanding of the means he has placed at our disposal for attaining that salvation. God "wants all to be saved, and to come to the knowledge of the truth" *(1 Tim 2:4),* and that truth is nothing other than Jesus Christ, eternal Son of the Father, who has reconciled all things in himself by the power of his Cross. In fidelity to the Lord's will, as expressed in that passage from St Paul's First Letter to Timothy, we recognise that the Church is called to be inclusive, yet never at the expense of Christian truth. Herein lies the dilemma facing all who are genuinely committed to the ecumenical journey.

In the figure of John Henry Newman, who is to be beatified on Sunday, we celebrate a churchman whose ecclesial vision was nurtured by his Anglican background and matured during his many years of ordained ministry in the Church of England. He can teach us the virtues that ecumenism demands: on the one hand, he was moved to follow his conscience, even at great personal cost; and on the other hand, the warmth of his continued friendship with his former colleagues led him to explore with them, in a truly eirenical spirit, the questions on which they differed, driven by a deep longing for unity in faith. Your Grace, in that same spirit of friendship, let us renew our determination to pursue the goal of unity in faith, hope, and love, in accordance with the will of our one Lord and Saviour Jesus Christ.

With these sentiments, I take my leave of you. May the grace of the Lord Jesus Christ and the love of God and the fellowship of the Holy Spirit be with you all *(2 Cor 13:13).* ■

A joint statement issued after the Pope and Archbishop's private meeting said, "They affirmed the need to proclaim the Gospel message of salvation in Jesus Christ, both in a reasoned and convincing way in the contemporary context of profound cultural and social transformation, and in lives of holiness and transparency to God."

It also said, "They agreed on the importance of improving ecumenical relations and continuing theological dialogue in the face of new challenges to unity from within the Christian community and beyond it."

Pope Benedict's address to Politicians, Diplomats, Academics and Business Leaders

Westminster Hall, City of Westminster, Friday, 17th September 2010. 7:10pm

Mr Speaker,

Thank you for your words of welcome on behalf of this distinguished gathering. As I address you, I am conscious of the privilege afforded me to speak to the British people and their representatives in Westminster Hall, a building of unique significance in the civil and political history of the people of these islands. Allow me also to express my esteem for the Parliament which has existed on this site for centuries and which has had such a profound influence on the development of participative government among the nations, especially in the Commonwealth and the English-speaking world at large. Your common law tradition serves as the basis of legal systems in many parts of the world, and your particular vision of the respective rights and duties of the state and the individual, and of the separation of powers, remains an inspiration to many across the globe.

As I speak to you in this historic setting, I think of the countless men and women down the centuries who have played their part in the momentous events that have taken place within these walls and have shaped the lives of many generations of Britons, and others besides. In particular, I recall the figure of St Thomas More, the great English scholar and statesman, who is admired by believers and non-believers alike for the integrity with which he followed his conscience, even at the cost of displeasing the sovereign whose "good servant" he was, because he chose to serve God first. The dilemma which faced More in those difficult times, the perennial question of the relationship between what is owed to Caesar and what is owed to God, allows me the opportunity to reflect with you briefly on the proper place of religious belief within the political process.

This country's Parliamentary tradition owes much to the national instinct for moderation, to the desire to achieve a genuine balance between the legitimate claims of government and the rights of those subject to it. While decisive steps have been taken at several points in your history to place limits on the exercise of power, the nation's political institutions have been able to evolve with a remarkable degree of stability. In the process, Britain has emerged as a pluralist democracy which places great value on freedom of speech, freedom of political affiliation and respect for the rule of law, with a strong sense of the individual's

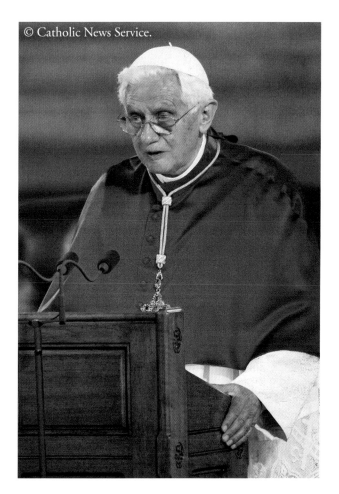

© Catholic News Service.

rights and duties, and of the equality of all citizens before the law. While couched in different language, Catholic social teaching has much in common with this approach, in its overriding concern to safeguard the unique dignity of every human person, created in the image and likeness of God, and in its emphasis on the duty of civil authority to foster the common good.

And yet the fundamental questions at stake in Thomas More's trial continue to present themselves in ever-changing terms as new social conditions emerge. Each generation, as it seeks to advance the common good, must ask anew: what are the requirements that governments may reasonably impose upon citizens, and how far do they extend? By appeal to what authority can moral dilemmas be resolved? These questions take us directly to the   >

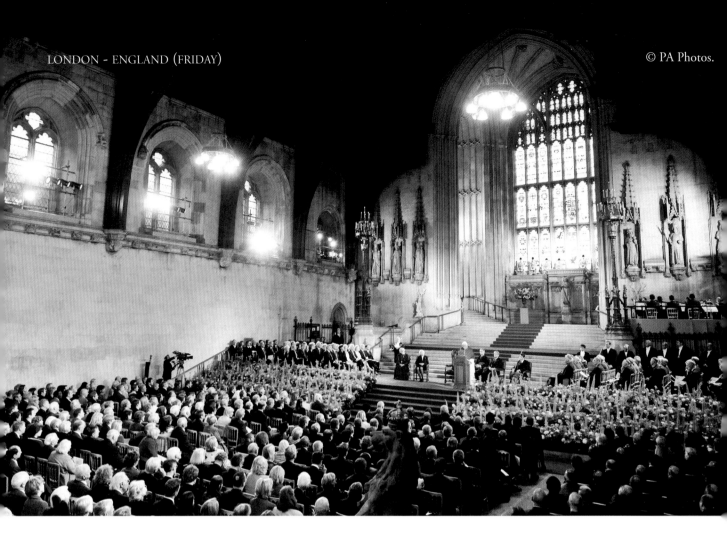

ethical foundations of civil discourse. If the moral principles underpinning the democratic process are themselves determined by nothing more solid than social consensus, then the fragility of the process becomes all too evident - herein lies the real challenge for democracy.

The inadequacy of pragmatic, short-term solutions to complex social and ethical problems has been illustrated all too clearly by the recent global financial crisis. There is widespread agreement that the lack of a solid ethical foundation for economic activity has contributed to the grave difficulties now being experienced by millions of people throughout the world. Just as "every economic decision has a moral consequence" *(Caritas in Veritate, 37),* so too in the political field, the ethical dimension of policy has far-reaching consequences that no government can afford to ignore. A positive illustration of this is found in one of the British Parliament's particularly notable achievements – the abolition of the slave trade. The campaign that led to this landmark legislation was built upon firm ethical principles, rooted in the natural law, and it has made a contribution to civilisation of which this nation may be justly proud.

The central question at issue, then, is this: where is the ethical foundation for political choices to be found? The Catholic tradition maintains that the objective norms governing right action are accessible to reason, prescinding from the content of revelation. According to this understanding, the role of religion in political debate is not so much to supply these norms, as if they could not be known by non-believers – still less to propose concrete political solutions, which would lie altogether outside the competence of religion – but rather to help purify and shed light upon the application of reason to the discovery of objective moral principles. This "corrective" role of religion vis-à-vis reason is not always welcomed though, partly because distorted forms of religion, such as sectarianism and fundamentalism, can be seen to create serious social problems themselves. And in their turn, these distortions of religion arise when insufficient attention is given to the purifying and structuring role of reason within religion. It is a two-way process. Without the corrective supplied by religion though, reason too can fall prey to distortions, as when it is manipulated by ideology, or applied in a partial way that fails to take full account of the dignity of the human person. Such misuse of reason, after all, was what gave rise to the slave trade in the first place and to many other social evils, not least the totalitarian ideologies of the 20th century. This is why I would suggest that the world of reason and the world of faith – the world of secular rationality and the world of religious belief – need one another and should not be afraid to enter into a profound and ongoing dialogue, for the good of our civilisation.

Religion, in other words, is not a problem for legislators to solve, but a vital contributor to the national conversation. In this light, I cannot but voice my concern at the increasing marginalisation of

> I recall the figure of St Thomas More, the great English scholar and statesman, who is admired by believers and non-believers alike for the integrity with which he followed his conscience, even at the cost of displeasing the sovereign whose 'good servant' he was, because he chose to serve God first.

religion, particularly of Christianity, that is taking place in some quarters, even in nations which place a great emphasis on tolerance. There are those who would advocate that the voice of religion be silenced, or at least relegated to the purely private sphere. There are those who argue that the public celebration of festivals such as Christmas should be discouraged, in the questionable belief that it might somehow offend those of other religions or none. And there are those who argue – paradoxically with the intention of eliminating discrimination – that Christians in public roles should be required at times to act against their conscience. These are worrying signs of a failure to appreciate not only the rights of believers to freedom of conscience and freedom of religion, but also the legitimate role of religion in the public square. I would invite all of you, therefore, within your respective spheres of influence, to seek ways of promoting and encouraging dialogue between faith and reason at every level of national life.

Your readiness to do so is already implied in the unprecedented invitation extended to me today. And it finds expression in the fields of concern in which your Government has been engaged with the Holy See. In the area of peace, there have been exchanges regarding the elaboration of an international arms trade treaty; regarding human rights, the Holy See and the United Kingdom have welcomed the spread of democracy, especially in the last 65 years; in the field of development, there has been collaboration on debt relief, fair trade and financing for development, particularly through the International Finance Facility, the International Immunisation Bond, and the Advanced Market Commitment. The Holy See also looks forward to exploring with the United Kingdom new ways to promote environmental responsibility, to the benefit of all.

I also note that the present Government has committed the United Kingdom to devoting 0.7% of national income to development aid by 2013. In recent years it has been encouraging to witness the positive signs of a worldwide growth in solidarity towards the poor. But to turn this solidarity into effective action calls for fresh thinking that will improve life conditions in many important areas, such as food production, clean water, job creation,

education, support to families, especially migrants, and basic healthcare. Where human lives are concerned, time is always short: yet the world has witnessed the vast resources that governments can draw upon to rescue financial institutions deemed "too big to fail". Surely the integral human development of the world's peoples is no less important: here is an enterprise, worthy of the world's attention, that is truly "too big to fail".

This overview of recent co-operation between the United Kingdom and the Holy See illustrates well how much progress has been made, in the years that have passed since the establishment of bilateral diplomatic relations, in promoting throughout the world the many core values that we share. I hope and pray that this relationship will continue to bear fruit, and that it will be mirrored in a growing acceptance of the need for dialogue and respect at every level of society between the world of reason and the world of faith. I am convinced that, within this country too, there are many areas in which the Church and the public authorities can work together for the good of citizens, in harmony with this Parliament's historic practice of invoking the Spirit's guidance upon those who seek to improve the conditions of all mankind. For such co-operation to be possible, religious bodies – including institutions linked to the Catholic Church – need to be free to act in accordance with their own principles and specific convictions based upon the faith and the official teaching of the Church. In this way, such basic rights as religious freedom, freedom of conscience and freedom of association are guaranteed. The angels looking down on us from the magnificent ceiling of this ancient Hall remind us of the long tradition from which British Parliamentary democracy has evolved. They remind us that God is constantly watching over us to guide and protect us. And they summon us to acknowledge the vital contribution that religious belief has made and can continue to make to the life of the nation.

Mr Speaker, I thank you once again for this opportunity briefly to address this distinguished audience. Let me assure you and the Lord Speaker of my continued good wishes and prayers for you and for the fruitful work of both Houses of this ancient Parliament. Thank you and God bless you all! ∎

Pope Benedict's addresses at the Ecumenical Celebration

Westminster Abbey, Friday 17th September 2010. 7:10pm

INTRODUCTORY WORDS OF HIS HOLINESS BENEDICT XVI DURING THE EVENING PRAYER

Your Grace, Mr Dean, Dear Friends in Christ,

I thank you for your gracious welcome. This noble edifice evokes England's long history, so deeply marked by the preaching of the Gospel and the Christian culture to which it gave birth. I come here today as a pilgrim from Rome, to pray before the tomb of St Edward the Confessor and to join you in imploring the gift of Christian unity. May these moments of prayer and friendship confirm us in love for Jesus Christ, our Lord and Saviour, and in common witness to the enduring power of the Gospel to illumine the future of this great nation.

ADDRESS OF THE HOLY FATHER AT THE CONCLUSION OF THE EVENING PRAYER

Dear friends in Christ,

I thank the Lord for this opportunity to join you, the representatives of the Christian confessions present in Great Britain, in this magnificent Abbey Church dedicated to St Peter, whose architecture and history speak so eloquently of our common heritage of faith. Here we cannot help but be reminded of how greatly the Christian faith shaped the unity and culture of Europe and the heart and spirit of the English people. Here too, we are forcibly reminded that what we share, in Christ, is greater than what continues to divide us.

(above) Pope Benedict XVI arrives at Westminster Abbey, London, where he is greeted by the Dean of Westminster, the Right Reverend Dr. John Hall. © www.papalvisit.org.uk

(opposite) Pope Benedict XVI prays with the Archbishop of Canterbury, Dr. Rowan Williams, in the Shrine of St Edward the Confessor in Westminster Abbey, London. © PA Photos.

I am grateful to His Grace the Archbishop of Canterbury for his kind greeting, and to the Dean and Chapter of this venerable abbey for their cordial welcome. I thank the Lord for allowing me, as the Successor of St Peter in the See of Rome, to make this pilgrimage to the tomb of St Edward the Confessor. Edward, King of England, remains a model of Christian witness and an example of that true grandeur to which the Lord summons his disciples in the Scriptures we have just heard: the grandeur of a humility and obedience grounded in Christ's own example *(cf. Phil 2:6-8),* the grandeur of a fidelity which does not hesitate to embrace the mystery of the Cross out of undying love for the divine Master and unfailing hope in his promises *(cf. Mk 10:43-44).*

This year, as we know, marks the hundredth anniversary of the modern ecumenical movement, which began with the Edinburgh Conference's appeal for Christian unity as the prerequisite for a credible and convincing witness to the Gospel in our time. In commemorating this anniversary, we must give thanks for the remarkable progress made towards this noble goal through the efforts of committed Christians of every denomination. At the same time, however, we remain conscious of how much yet remains to be done. In a world marked by growing interdependence and solidarity, we are challenged to proclaim with renewed conviction the reality of our reconciliation and liberation in Christ, and to propose the truth of the Gospel as the key to an authentic and integral human development. In a society which has become increasingly indifferent or even hostile to the Christian message, we are all the more compelled to give a joyful and convincing account of the hope that is within us *(cf. 1 Pet 3:15),* and to present the Risen Lord as the response to the deepest questions and spiritual aspirations of the men and women of our time.

As we processed to the chancel at the beginning of this service, the choir sang that Christ is our 'sure foundation'. He is the Eternal Son of God, of one substance with the Father, who took flesh, as the Creed states, "for us men and for our salvation". He alone has the words of everlasting life. In him, as the Apostle teaches, "all things hold together" ... "for in him all the fullness of God was pleased to dwell" *(Col 1:17,19).*

Our commitment to Christian unity is born of nothing less than our faith in Christ, in this Christ, risen >

from the dead and seated at the right hand of the Father, who will come again in glory to judge the living and the dead. It is the reality of Christ's person, his saving work and above all the historical fact of his resurrection, which is the content of the apostolic kerygma and those credal formulas which, beginning in the New Testament itself, have guaranteed the integrity of its transmission. The Church's unity, in a word, can never be other than a unity in the apostolic faith, in the faith entrusted to each new member of the Body of Christ during the rite of Baptism. It is this faith which unites us to the Lord, makes us sharers in his Holy Spirit, and thus, even now, sharers in the life of the Blessed Trinity, the model of the Church's koinonia here below.

Dear friends, we are all aware of the challenges, the blessings, the disappointments and the signs of hope which have marked our ecumenical journey. Tonight we entrust all of these to the Lord, confident in his providence and the power of his grace. We know that the friendships we have forged, the dialogue which we have begun and the hope which guides us will provide strength and direction as we persevere on our common journey. At the same time, with evangelical realism, we must also recognise the challenges which confront us, not only along the path of Christian unity, but also in our task of proclaiming Christ in our day. Fidelity to the word of God, precisely because it is a true word, demands of us an obedience which leads us together to a deeper understanding of the Lord's will, an obedience which must be free of intellectual conformism or facile accommodation to the spirit of the age. This is the word of encouragement which I wish to leave with you this evening, and I do so in fidelity to my ministry as the Bishop of Rome and the Successor of St Peter, charged with a particular care for the unity of Christ's flock.

Gathered in this ancient monastic church, we can recall the example of a great Englishman and churchman whom we honour in common: St Bede the Venerable. At the dawn of a new age in the life of society and of the Church, Bede understood both the importance of fidelity to the word of God as transmitted by the apostolic tradition, and the need for creative openness to new developments and to the demands of a sound implantation of the Gospel in contemporary language and culture.

This nation, and the Europe which Bede and his contemporaries helped to build, once again stands at the threshold of a new age. May St Bede's example inspire the Christians of these lands to rediscover their shared legacy, to strengthen what they have in common, and to continue their efforts to grow in friendship. May the Risen Lord strengthen our efforts to mend the ruptures of the past and to meet the challenges of the present with hope in the future which, in his providence, he holds out to us and to our world. Amen. ■

Anglican Archbishop Rowan Williams of Canterbury and Pope Benedict XVI are pictured at Evening Prayer at Westminster Abbey in London. © Catholic News Service.

Archbishop Williams welcomed Pope Benedict as the first pope ever to visit Westminster Abbey, which was home to a community of Catholic Benedictine monks until 1540 when King Henry VIII dissolved the monastic community.

Archbishop of Canterbury's address at Evening Prayer

Westminster Abbey, Friday 17th September 2010. 7:30pm

Your Holiness, Members of the Collegiate Body, distinguished guests, brothers and sisters in Christ:
Christians in Britain, especially in England, look back with the most fervent gratitude to the events of 597, when Augustine landed on these shores to preach the gospel to the Anglo-Saxons at the behest of Pope St Gregory the Great. For Christians of all traditions and confessions, St Gregory is a figure of compelling attractiveness and spiritual authority – pastor and leader, scholar and exegete and spiritual guide. The fact that the first preaching of the Gospel to the English peoples in the sixth and seventh centuries has its origins in his vision creates a special connection for us with the See of the Apostles Peter and Paul; and Gregory's witness and legacy remain an immensely fruitful source of inspiration for our own mission in these dramatically different times. Two dimensions of that vision may be of special importance as we reflect today on the significance of Your Holiness's visit to us.

St Gregory was the first to spell out for the faithful something of the magnitude of the gift given to Christ's Church through the life of St Benedict – to whom you, Your Holiness, have signalled your devotion in the choice of your name as Pope. In St Gregory's *Dialogues*, we can trace the impact of St Benedict – an extraordinary man who, through a relatively brief Rule of life, opened up for the whole civilisation of Europe since the sixth century the possibility of living in joy and mutual service, in simplicity and self-denial, in a balanced pattern of labour and prayer in which every moment spoke of human dignity fully realised in surrender to a loving God. The Benedictine life proved a sure foundation not only for generations of monks and nuns, but for an entire culture in which productive work and contemplative silence and receptivity – human dignity and human freedom – were both honoured.

Our own culture, a culture in which so often it seems that 'love has grown cold', is one in which we can see the dehumanising effects of losing sight of Benedict's vision. Work is so often an anxious and obsessive matter, as if our whole value as human beings depended upon it; and so, consequently, unemployment, still a scourge and a threat in these uncertain financial times, comes to seem like a loss of dignity and meaning in life. We live in an age where there is a desperate need to recover the sense of the dignity of both labour and leisure and the necessity of a silent openness to God that allows our true character to grow and flourish by participating in an eternal love.

In a series of profound and eloquent encyclicals, you have explored these themes for our day, grounding everything in the eternal love of the Holy Trinity, challenging us to hope both for this world and the next, and analysing the ways in which our economic habits have trapped us in a reductive and unworthy style of human living. In this building with its long Benedictine legacy, we acknowledge with gratitude your contribution to a Benedictine vision for our days, and pray that your time with us in Britain may help us all towards a renewal of the hope and energy we need as Christians to witness to our conviction that in their relation to God men and women may grow into the fullest freedom and beauty of spirit.

And in this, we are recalled also to the importance among the titles of the Bishops of Rome of St Gregory's own self-designation as 'servant of the servants of God' – surely the one title that points most directly to the example of the Lord who has called us. There is, we know, no authority in the Church that is not the authority of service: that is, of building up the people of God to full maturity. Christ's service is simply the way in which we meet his almighty power: the power to remake the world he has created, pouring out into our lives, individually and together, what we truly need in order to become fully what we are made to be – the image of the divine life. It is that image which the pastor in the Church seeks to serve, bowing down in reverence before each human person in the knowledge of the glory for which he or she was made.

Christians have very diverse views about the nature of the vocation that belongs to the See of Rome. Yet, as Your Holiness's great predecessor reminded us all in his encyclical *Ut Unum Sint,* we must learn to reflect together on how the historic ministry of the Roman Church and its chief pastor may speak to the Church catholic – East and West, global north and global south of the authority of Christ and his apostles to build up the Body in love; how it may be realised as a ministry of patience and reverence towards all, a ministry of creative love and self-giving that leads us all into the same path of seeking not our own comfort or profit but the good of the entire human community and the glory of God the creator and redeemer.

We pray that your time with us will be a further step for all of us into the mystery of the cross and the resurrection, so that growing together we may become more effective channels for God's purpose to heal the wounds of humankind, and to restore once again both in our societies and our environment the likeness of his glory as revealed in the face of Jesus Christ. ∎

© **Rowan Williams 2010**

Pope meets privately with British government leaders

Pope Benedict XVI meets with Prime Minister David Cameron, (1) Deputy Prime Minister Nick Clegg (2) and Acting Labour leader Harriet Harman (3) at Archbishop's House, near Westminster Cathedral in central London. © PA Photos.

Pope Benedict XVI met privately with British government leaders during his visit to London, a day after telling the country's top political and cultural leaders that Christianity cannot be marginalised.

No details were available of the pontiff's 20-minute talk with Prime Minister David Cameron in the official residence of the Catholic Archbishop of Westminster.

The head of government, whose Conservative Party triumphed in May elections, attended the funeral of his stockbroker father, Ian Cameron, on the 17th September, and missed other events during the Pope's visit to the British capital.

The Pope also held brief talks with Deputy Prime Minister Nick Clegg, who was accompanied by his wife and children, and the acting head of the opposition Labour Party, Harriet Harman, who earlier defended Britain's controversial equalities law after criticism by the Pope.

Speaking later, Harman said she had welcomed

Pope Benedict on behalf of the Labour Party, adding that she had talked with the pontiff about the "long, close connection – and leading role played by – Catholics in the Labour Party over many decades."

"We talked about the many struggles for social justice that the Catholics and the Labour Party have struggled on together," Harman told journalists outside Archbishop's House. "We also discussed the challenges that still remain here and abroad."

The morning meetings took place shortly before the Pope celebrated Mass in the adjoining Catholic Westminster Cathedral.

The previous night, British government ministers hosted a dinner for members of the Vatican delegation, headed by the secretary of state, Cardinal Tarcisio Bertone. Pope Benedict did not attend the dinner.

An official statement said both sides had discussed a "range of areas of shared interest" at the London dinner, including a joint commitment to end poverty and underdevelopment.

The statement said the British government, represented by Foreign Secretary William Hague, concurred with the Vatican on the need to fight "unnecessary suffering caused by hunger, diseases and illiteracy," as well as for urgent action to counter climate change and to "rapidly reduce greenhouse gas emissions, set in motion the transition to a global low-carbon economy, and assist poor and vulnerable countries to adapt to the impacts of climate change that are already inevitable."

"Strong political leadership and respect for the ethos of local communities are necessary in the promotion of the right to life, food, health and development for all," the statement said. ■

By Jonathan Luxmoore

Archbishop Nichols' welcome address

Westminster Cathedral, Saturday 18th September 2010. 10:45am

Most Holy Father,
It is difficult to find words to express our joy and happiness at your presence here among us. You are most welcome.

I know I speak for everyone in this great congregation, drawn from every diocese in our countries and for so many who are participating by radio and television as I express these words of greeting.

Holy Father, we offer you our love and prayers to help and sustain you in your ministry as the successor of St Peter. Your ministry is a great gift to us for the Lord asks you to strengthen and nourish us, His people. That is what you do, being a sign and servant of the unity of the whole Church. Standing in the shoes of the Fisherman is demanding. So we give you our loving loyalty and sincere devotion.

Today we are full of joy that you lead us in the celebration of the Holy Mass in this Cathedral of the Most Precious Blood of our Saviour. We come to Him because we know we stand in need of His forgiveness and healing. Wonderfully we find these gifts opened for us in his death on the Cross. For in dying, He, who alone is God in our flesh, destroys every death that threatens us and restores our life. This is our faith, the faith of the Church, the faith which you affirm and proclaim with such authority, integrity and eloquence.

Holy Father, thank you for coming to be with us. Please lead us to the Lord, in Word and Sacrament, that He may strengthen and renew us. ■

Archbishop Vincent Nichols. President of the Bishops' Conference of England and Wales

Pope Benedict's Westminster Cathedral Homily

Westminster Cathedral, Saturday 18th September 2010. 11:00am

Dear Friends in Christ,

I greet all of you with joy in the Lord and I thank you for your warm reception. I am grateful to Archbishop Nichols for his words of welcome on your behalf. Truly, in this meeting of the Successor of Peter and the faithful of Britain, **"heart speaks unto heart"** as we rejoice in the love of Christ and in our common profession of the Catholic faith which comes to us from the Apostles. I am especially happy that our meeting takes place in this cathedral dedicated to the Most Precious Blood, which is the sign of God's redemptive mercy poured out upon the world through the passion, death and resurrection of his Son, our Lord Jesus Christ. In a particular way I greet the Archbishop of Canterbury, who honours us by his presence.

The visitor to this cathedral cannot fail to be struck by the great crucifix dominating the nave, which portrays Christ's body, crushed by suffering, overwhelmed by sorrow, the innocent victim whose death has reconciled us with the Father and given us a share in the very life of God. The Lord's outstretched arms seem to embrace this entire church, lifting up to the Father all the ranks of the faithful who gather around the altar of the Eucharistic sacrifice and share in its fruits. The crucified Lord stands above and before us as the source of our life and salvation, "the high priest of the good things to come", as the author of the Letter to the Hebrews calls him in today's first reading *(Heb 9:11).*

It is in the shadow, so to speak, of this striking image, that I would like to consider the word of God which has been proclaimed in our midst and reflect on the mystery of the Precious Blood. For that mystery leads us to see the unity between Christ's sacrifice on the Cross, the Eucharistic sacrifice which he has given to his Church, and his eternal priesthood, whereby, seated at the right hand of the Father, he makes unceasing intercession for us, the members of his mystical body.

Let us begin with the sacrifice of the Cross. The outpouring of Christ's blood is the source of the Church's life. St John, as we know, sees in the water and blood which flowed from Our Lord's body the wellspring of that divine life which is bestowed by the Holy Spirit and communicated to us in the sacraments *(Jn 19:34; cf. 1 Jn1:7; 5:6-7).* The Letter to the Hebrews draws out, we might say, the liturgical implications of this mystery. Jesus, by his suffering and death, his self-oblation in the eternal Spirit, has become our high priest and "the mediator of a new covenant" *(Heb 9:15).* These words echo Our Lord's own words at the Last Supper, when he instituted the Eucharist as the sacrament of his body, given up for us, and his blood, the blood of the new and everlasting covenant shed for the forgiveness of sins *(cf. Mk 14:24; Mt26:28; Lk 22:20).*

Faithful to Christ's command to "do this in memory of me" *(Lk 22:19),* the Church in every time and place celebrates the Eucharist until the Lord returns in glory, rejoicing in his sacramental presence and drawing upon the power of his saving sacrifice for the redemption of the world. The reality of the Eucharistic sacrifice has always been at the heart of Catholic faith; called into question in the 16th century, it was solemnly reaffirmed at the Council of Trent against the backdrop of our justification in Christ. Here in England, as we know, there were many who staunchly defended the Mass, often at great cost, giving rise to that devotion to the Most Holy Eucharist which has been a hallmark of Catholicism in these lands.

The Eucharistic sacrifice of the Body and Blood of Christ embraces in turn the mystery of Our Lord's continuing passion in the members of his Mystical Body, the Church in every age. Here the great crucifix which towers above us serves as a reminder that   **>**

The visitor to this Cathedral cannot fail to be struck by the great crucifix dominating the nave, which portrays Christ's body, crushed by suffering, overwhelmed by sorrow, the innocent victim whose death has reconciled us with the Father and given us a share in the very life of God. The Lord's outstretched arms seem to embrace this entire church, lifting up to the Father all the ranks of the faithful who gather around the altar of the Eucharistic sacrifice and share in its fruits.

Christ, our eternal high priest, daily unites our own sacrifices, our own sufferings, our own needs, hopes and aspirations, to the infinite merits of his sacrifice. Through him, with him, and in him, we lift up our own bodies as a sacrifice holy and acceptable to God *(cf. Rom 12:1)*. In this sense we are caught up in his eternal oblation, completing, as St Paul says, in our flesh what is lacking in Christ's afflictions for the sake of his body, the Church *(cf. Col 1:24)*. In the life of the Church, in her trials and tribulations, Christ continues, in the stark phrase of Pascal, to be in agony until the end of the world *(Pensées, 553, éd. Brunschvicg)*.

We see this aspect of the mystery of Christ's precious blood represented, most eloquently, by the martyrs of every age, who drank from the cup which Christ himself drank, and whose own blood, shed in union with his sacrifice, gives new life to the Church. It is also reflected in our brothers and sisters throughout the world who even now are suffering discrimination and persecution for their Christian faith. Yet it is also present, often hidden in the suffering of all those individual Christians who daily unite their sacrifices to those of the Lord for the sanctification of the Church and the redemption of the world. My thoughts go in a special way to all those who are spiritually united with this Eucharistic celebration, and in particular the sick, the elderly, the handicapped and those who suffer mentally and spiritually.

Here too I think of the immense suffering caused by the abuse of children, especially within the Church and by her ministers. Above all, I express my deep sorrow to the innocent victims of these unspeakable crimes, along with my hope that the power of Christ's grace, his sacrifice of reconciliation, will bring deep healing and peace to their lives. I also acknowledge, with you, the shame and humiliation which all of us have suffered because of these sins; and I invite you to offer it to the Lord with trust that this chastisement will contribute to the healing of the victims, the purification of the Church and the renewal of her age-old commitment to the education and care of young people. I express my gratitude for the efforts being made to address this problem responsibly, and I ask all of you to show your concern for the victims and solidarity with your priests.

Dear friends, let us return to the contemplation of the great crucifix which rises above us. Our Lord's hands, extended on the Cross, also invite us to contemplate our participation in his eternal priesthood and thus our responsibility, as members of his body, to bring the reconciling power of his sacrifice to the world in which we live. The Second Vatican Council spoke eloquently of the indispensable role of the laity in carrying forward the Church's mission through their efforts to serve as a leaven of the Gospel in society and to work for the advancement of God's Kingdom in the world *(cf. Lumen Gentium, 31; Apostolicam Actuositatem, 7)*. The Council's appeal to the lay faithful to take up their baptismal sharing in Christ's mission echoed the insights and teachings of John Henry Newman. May the profound ideas of this great Englishman continue to inspire all Christ's followers in this land to conform their every thought, word and action to Christ, and to work strenuously to defend those unchanging moral truths which, taken up, illuminated and confirmed by the Gospel, stand at the foundation of a truly humane, just and free society.

How much contemporary society needs this witness! How much we need, in the Church and in society, witnesses of the beauty of holiness, witnesses of the splendour of truth, witnesses of the joy and freedom born of a living relationship with Christ! One of the greatest challenges facing us today is how to speak convincingly of the wisdom and liberating power of God's word to a world which all too often sees the Gospel as a constriction of human freedom, instead of the truth which liberates our minds and enlightens our efforts to live wisely and well, both as individuals and as members of society.

Let us pray, then, that the Catholics of this land will become ever more conscious of their dignity as a priestly people, called to consecrate the world to God through lives of faith and holiness. And may this increase of apostolic zeal be accompanied by an outpouring of prayer for vocations to the ordained priesthood. For the more the lay apostolate grows, the more urgently the need for priests is felt; and the more the laity's own sense of vocation is deepened, the more what is proper to the priest stands out. May many young men in this land find the strength to answer the Master's call to the ministerial priesthood, devoting their lives, their energy and their talents to God, thus building up his people in unity and fidelity to the Gospel, especially through the celebration of the Eucharistic sacrifice.

Dear friends, in this Cathedral of the Most Precious Blood, I invite you once more to look to Christ, who leads us in our faith and brings it to perfection *(cf. Heb 12:2)*. I ask you to unite yourselves ever more fully to the Lord, sharing in his sacrifice on the Cross and offering him that "spiritual worship" *(Rom 12:1)* which embraces every aspect of our lives and finds expression in our efforts to contribute to the coming of his Kingdom. I pray that, in doing so, you may join the ranks of faithful believers throughout the long Christian history of this land in building a society truly worthy of man, worthy of your nation's highest traditions. ∎

Official Pope Benedict XVI Commemorative Spoon

Celebrate the September visit of our Holy Father Pope Benedict XVI with this expertly crafted commemorative spoon.

Pope Benedict XVI visited the United Kingdom in September 2010, in what was the first papal UK visit since that of John Paul II in 1982. Remember this momentous occasion with this incredible spoon, adorned with the image of Pope Benedict XVI. Ornately decorated this spoon is coated gold and presented in a small spoon box. The spoon is marked with a Vaughtons stamp.

Since 1819, Vaughtons has been synonymous in the art of commemorative spoon manufacture. Using techniques developed over almost 200 years we are able to offer you this quite superb spoon. This piece has been designed by our artist Peter C. who has designed and created many famous works of art throughout the commemorating world.

* For Sterling Silver or 9 Carat Gold prices please enquire

yours for just
£4.95*
plus £1.60 p&p

Presented in a small spoon box with official Papal Visit 2010 crest

How to order

Visit: www.vaughtons.com
Call: 0121 554 9817 / 0121 554 0032
Post: Vaughtons, 16 Well Street, Birmingham B19 3BJ

Please send a cheque for £6.55 made payable to Vaughtons with your name, delivery address, telephone number and "Papal Single Spoon Offer" clearly marked on the reverse.

LONDON - ENGLAND (SATURDAY)

Young people surround Pope Benedict XVI outside
Westminster Cathedral. © Catholic News Service.

Welcome to the Holy Father, on behalf of the young people of England, Wales and Scotland

Westminster Cathedral, Saturday 18th September 2010. 12:00pm

Dear Holy Father,

It is a privilege and a great pleasure to welcome you on behalf of young Catholics from England, Wales and Scotland. Your visit brings us together – it is like a family reunion - and we are very pleased to see you.

My name is Paschal Uche and I am from St Francis' Parish in East London. Gathered here today are 2,500 young people representing almost every parish in the country. Like many here I have been actively involved in the Church, serving the elderly in Lourdes and going on retreat. I know that others help in Confirmation sessions, parish music groups, youth groups, and projects serving those who are disadvantaged. We are a truly living Church that offers great opportunities for young people to encounter the love of Christ and share it.

Pope John Paul II said that our faith is a "noble and authentic adventure" and we really want other young people to experience this. It is our prayer that your visit inspires us to be "saints of the third millennium."

Holy Father we would like to ask you to bless for us a candle stand, which we hope will be a symbol for Catholic Youth Ministry. It has been thoughtfully designed for use in prayer, teaching and meditation.

For many of us before today you were a face on the television or a picture in a church but today we behold you face to face and on behalf of the Catholic youth of this great nation I would like to express my profound and heartfelt gratitude for your visit. May God Bless you. ∎

Paschal Uche (second left) welcomes Pope Benedict XVI, on behalf of Britain's young people, as the Pope sit on the steps of Westminster Cathedral, after celebrating Mass. © PA Photos.

Pope Benedict's Message to Young People

Piazza, Westminster Cathedral, Saturday 18th September 2010. 12:10pm

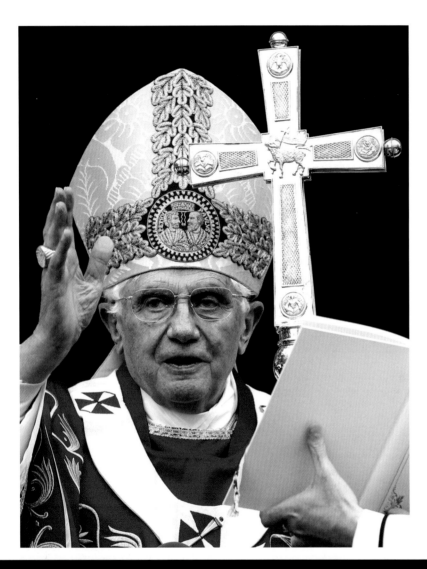

Mr Uche, Dear young friends, thank you for your warm welcome.
Heart Speaks unto heart, as you know I chose these words so dear to Cardinal Newman as the theme of my visit. In these few moments that we are together I wish to speak to you from my own heart, and I ask you to open your hearts to what I have to say.

I ask each of you first and foremost to look into your own heart, think of all the love that your heart was made to receive, and also love it is meant to give, after all we were made for love. This is what the Bible means when it says that we are made in the image and likeness of God. We were made to know the God of love, the God who is Father, Son and Holy Spirit, and to find our supreme fulfilment in that Divine love that knows no beginning or end.

We were made to receive love, and we have. Every day we should thank God for the love we have already known. For the love that has made us who we are. The love that is shown us what is truly important in life. We need to thank the Lord for the love we have received from our families, our friends, our teachers, and all those people in our lives who have helped

Pilgrim's reaction

I have been talking to one of the young people who was in the Piazza this morning at Westminster. She, and hundreds (well, 2000) of others are all having a picnic in Hyde Park before they come into the arena for the vigil. Fiona is representing her parish in Cockermouth, Cumbria, in the Diocese of Lancaster. She left home yesterday, and texted me from Preston around midnight. I asked her what her impressions were so far and she spoke of her joy and delight at seeing so many young Catholics gathered together from all over the country. Two thousand is just a

figure, but when you see them all gathered together in colour-coded sweatshirts, it is a very impressive sight.

I was so thrilled to hear Paschal Uche speak in front of everyone, as he welcomed the Pope. I cannot do justice to his wonderful words, his seemingly relaxed manner, his enthusiasm for what young people can do for the Church. It was the most uplifting moment of the day, so far, for me, notwithstanding the tremendously inspiring Mass that I had just attended.

Our young people are our greatest treasure. The Pope genuinely seemed reluctant to leave them.

http://thepapalvisit.wordpress.com/

us to realise how precious we are in their eyes, and in the eyes of God.

We were also made to give love, to make it the inspirational for all we do, and the most enduring thing in our lives. At times it seems so natural, especially when we feel the exhilaration of love, when our hearts brim over with generosity, idealism, the desire to help others to build a better world – but at other times, we realise it is difficult to love. Our hearts can easily be hardened by selfishness, envy and pride. The Blessed Mother Theresa of Calcutta, the great Missionary of Charity reminded us that giving love, pure and generous love, is the fruit of a daily decision.

Every day we have to choose to love and this requires help. The help that comes from Christ, from the wisdom found in his word. And from the Grace which he bestows us in the sacraments of his Church. This is the message I want to share with you today. I ask you to look into your hearts, each day, to find the source of all true love. Jesus is always there. Quietly waiting for us to bc still with him and to hear his

voice. Deep within your heart, he is calling you to spend time with him in prayer, but this kind of prayer, real prayer, requires discipline.

It requires time for moments of silence every day. Often it means waiting for the Lord to speak.

Even amidst the business and stress of our daily lives we need to make space for silence, because it is in silence that we find God. And in silence that we discover our true self.

And in discovering our true self we discover the particular vocation which God has given us for the building up of his church and the redemption of our world. **Heart speaks unto heart.** With these words from my heart, dear young friends, this is words from my heart.I assure you of my prayers for you.

That our lives will bear fruit of the cross, of the civilisation of the cross, I ask you to pray for me, for my Ministry as the successor of Peter, and for the needs of the Church throughout the world. Upon you, your families and friends, I call on you God's blessing of wisdom, joy and peace. ■

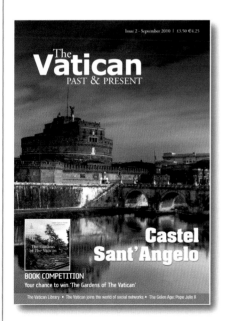

Bishop Regan's welcome to Pope Benedict from the people of Wales

Westminster Cathedral, Chapel of St Paul, Saturday 18th September 2010. 12:30pm

(below) Pope Benedict XVI sends a message to the people of Wales after lighting the candle of the statue of Our Lady of Cardigan.
© www.papalvisit.org.uk

(opposite) Blessing the latest addition to Westminster Cathedral, a mosaic of St David, the patron saint of Wales.
© www.papalvisit.org.uk

Your Holiness,
On behalf of the Catholics of Wales, and of Wales itself, I am immensely privileged to offer you our most sincere sentiments of loving respect and deep appreciation of all that you do for the building of God's Kingdom on earth.

Our joy that you are here in Britain is tempered by our disappointment that you cannot visit Wales on this occasion. But that regret is itself a sign of our esteem for you and your ministry of love in truth, Caritas in Veritate.

We are delighted that you are reaching out to Wales by lighting the candle held by Our Lady of Cardigan as she presents to us her Son as the light of the world.

That light is reflected to us by all those who have lived open to God's love, people who are represented by St David, the Patron of Wales. In blessing this mosaic dedicated to St David you remind modern Wales we must not forget the Christian values that formed this nation of Wales throughout its history.

Dad Sanctaidd, ar ran Catholigion Cymru, a Chymru ei hun, mae hi'n fraint arbennig iawn i mi allu cyflwyno i chi ein teimladau diffuant o barch cariadus, a gwerthfawrogiad dwys o'r hyn rydych chi'n ei gyflawni i adeiladu teyrnas Dduw ar y ddaear.

Mae ein llawenydd yn cael ei dymheru gan ein siom nad ydych yn gallu ymweld â Chymru y tro hwn. Ond mae'r siom hwnnw, ynddo'i hun, yn arwydd o'n hedmygedd ohonoch ac o'ch gweinidogaeth o gariad mewn gwirionedd, Caritas in Veritate.

Rydym yn falch iawn eich bod yn ymestyn tuag at Gymru trwy gynnau'r gannwyll a ddelir gan Ein Harglwyddes o Aberteifi wrth iddi gyflwyno'i Mab fel goleuni'r byd.

Mae'r goleuni hwnnw yn cael ei adlewyrchu atom gan bawb sydd wedi byw bywyd sy'n agored i gariad Duw, pobl a gynrychiolir gan Dewi Sant, Nawddsant ein gwlad. Wrth fendithio'r mosaig yma a gysegrir i Ddewi, rydych yn atgoffa Cymru heddiw na ddylem fyth anghofio'r gwerthoedd Cristnogol a ffurfiodd genedl y Cymry trwy gydol ei hanes.

[For the presentation of William Davies' book]
I have great pleasure in presenting to Your Holiness a striking reminder of those who have gone before us. Blessed William Davies wrote a book of Catholic devotion called *Y Drych Cristionogawl - The Christian Mirror,* which was the first book published in Wales. The romantic story of its being printed in a cave on a remote seashore has entered the folklore of Wales, and it speaks to us of a people who loved the Catholic Faith, and were prepared to sacrifice all for the one thing necessary, the love of God in truth.

This facsimile, printed this year, of a book printed in 1588 calls us to the same witness as we see in the lives of Blessed William Davies and the other Welsh martyrs, Catholic and Protestant. ∎

Message to the faithful of Wales

Westminster Cathedral, Chapel of St Paul, Saturday 18th September 2010. 12:30pm

Dear Bishop Regan,
Thank you for your very warm greeting on behalf of the faithful of Wales. I am happy to have this opportunity to honour the nation and its ancient Christian traditions by blessing a mosaic of St David, the patron saint of the Welsh people, and by lighting the candle of the statue of Our Lady of Cardigan.

St David was one of the great saints of the sixth century, that golden age of saints and missionaries in these isles, and he was thus a founder of the Christian culture which lies at the root of modern Europe. David's preaching was simple yet profound: his dying words to his monks were, "Be joyful, keep the faith, and do the little things". It is the little things that reveal our love for the one who loved us first *(cf. 1 Jn 4:19)* and that bind people into a community of faith, love and service. May St David's message, in all its simplicity and richness, continue to resound in Wales today, drawing the hearts of its people to renewed love for Christ and his Church.

Through the ages the Welsh people have been distinguished for their devotion to the Mother of God; this is evidenced by the innumerable places in Wales called 'Llanfair' – Mary's Church. As I prepare to light the candle held by Our Lady, I pray that she will continue to intercede with her Son for all the men and women of Wales. May the light of Christ continue to guide their steps and shape the life and culture of the nation.

Sadly, it was not possible for me to come to Wales during this visit. But I trust that this beautiful statue, which now returns to the National Shrine of Our Lady in Cardigan, will be a lasting reminder of the Pope's deep love for the Welsh people, and of his constant closeness, both in prayer and in the communion of the Church.

Bendith Duw ar bobol Cymru! God bless the people of Wales! ∎

Pope expresses sorrow, sense of shame to sex abuse victims

In a personal meeting with five victims of clerical sexual abuse, Pope Benedict XVI expressed his "deep sorrow and shame" over their suffering and promised the Church would do "all in its power" to investigate cases of abuse and safeguard the young.

The encounter took place just hours after the German pontiff, speaking at a Mass in Westminster Cathedral, denounced what he called the "unspeakable crimes" committed by some priests against young people.

The Vatican said in a statement that during the 30-minute meeting with victims, the 83-year-old Pope was "moved by what they had to say and expressed his deep sorrow and shame over what victims and their families had suffered."

"He prayed with them and assured them that the Catholic Church is continuing to implement effective measures designed to safeguard young people, and that it is doing all in its power to investigate allegations, to collaborate with civil authorities and to bring to justice clergy and religious accused of these egregious crimes," the statement said.

The group included four women and one man, all adults, who came from England, Scotland and Wales. Each had time to speak "with great intensity and emotion" about their suffering, the Vatican spokesman, Jesuit Fr. Federico Lombardi, told reporters.

He said the Pope prayed with them at the beginning and the end of the encounter; the only other people present were three people who work with abuse victims and a translator.

The Vatican said the Pope had "prayed that all the victims of abuse might experience healing and reconciliation, and be able to overcome their past and present distress with serenity and hope for the future."

Asked whether 30 minutes was enough time for the Pope to have given the victims, Bill Kilgallon, head of the National Catholic Safeguarding Commission, said: "It's longer than the prime minister got."

Although the encounter was unannounced, it had been widely expected. The Pope has previously met with abuse victims in the United States, Australia and Malta, and the Vatican has said such meetings are part of an effort to implement the Pope's own call for "absolute transparency" over sexual abuse and its commitment to reconciliation with victims.

Even as the London meeting took place, however, protesters in another part of the city – including some sex abuse victims – accused the Pope of protecting priests who have abused minors. Critics said the Pope's actions to date have failed to address the accountability issue in the Church.

Later in the afternoon, the Pope held an unscheduled meeting with the Church's child protection officers and said their efforts have helped ensure that allegations of abuse are dealt with "swiftly and justly."

"While there are never grounds for complacency, credit should be given where it is due: the efforts of the Church in this country and elsewhere, especially in the last 10 years, to guarantee the safety of children and

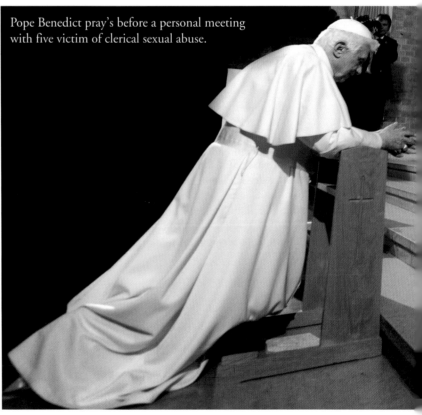

Pope Benedict pray's before a personal meeting with five victim of clerical sexual abuse.

young people and to show them every respect as they grow to maturity, should be acknowledged," he said.

In Britain, after dozens of priestly sex abuse cases came to light in the late 1990s, bishops adopted a series of measures to protect children, setting up a national office for child protection and encouraging the appointment of trained child protection officers in each parish and school. The bishops also made a commitment to turn every case of alleged child abuse over to the police.

On the plane carrying him to Great Britain, Pope Benedict said the Church was not vigilant enough or fast enough in responding to cases of sexual abuse.

"These revelations were for me a shock, and a great sadness. It is difficult to understand how this perversion of the priestly ministry was possible," he said. He said helping the victims overcome trauma was the Church's first priority, and said perpetrators must never be allowed access to children.

The Pope's comments have consistently drawn criticism from sex abuse victims' advocacy groups like the US -based Survivors Network of those Abused by Priests, known as SNAP. His remarks on the plane were also dismissed by critics.

"It's disingenuous to say Church officials have been slow and insufficiently vigilant in dealing with clergy sex crimes and cover ups. On the contrary, they've been prompt and vigilant, but in concealing, not preventing, these horrors," said Joelle Casteix in a statement published on the SNAP Website.

Among the relatively small number of protesters demonstrating against the Pope's visit in Britain, were those holding signs and banners that read: "Put the pope on trial" and "Pope, protector of pedophile priests."

The liturgy at Westminster Cathedral featured Latin and English-language prayers, and was attended by representatives of other Christian churches, including Anglican Archbishop Rowan Williams, who hosted the Pope the day before at the Anglican headquarters in London.

The Pope noted the giant crucifix that dominates the nave of the cathedral, and said this striking image and its connection with the Eucharistic sacrifice was at the heart of the Catholic faith.

"Here in England, as we know, there were many who staunchly defended the Mass, often at great cost, giving rise to that devotion to the most holy Eucharist," he said. ∎

By John Thavis

St Peter's welcomes the Pope

St Peter's Residence, Vauxhall, Saturday 18th September 2010. 5:21pm

Most Holy Father,
It is with great joy in our hearts that we say "Welcome Holy Father; welcome to St Peter's Residence". Our joy is born of gratitude and thanksgiving to God for the immense privilege that is ours today, and so, in the name of Mother General, the Little Sisters of the Poor and residents here at St Peter's and all over the world we assure you of our love, our deep affection and, above all, our prayers.

You have come in the name of Christ and his Church to confirm and strengthen us in our faith, so it is with eager anticipation that we await the message you are about to address to us.

It is in visiting your elderly brothers and sisters that you bear special witness to the immeasurable love of the Heart of Jesus for some of the most vulnerable and often frail members of today's society. Thank you, Holy Father, for including this visit to older people in your agenda. By doing so, you are underlining the real importance of caring for the elderly in our world of today.

Each elderly person has a vast experience of life, with their own story to tell. Often they have accumulated a great store of wisdom and strength of character and we know that the life of each one is precious in the eyes of God.

We are really happy to assure you, Holy Father, that each day here in St Peter's and in our Homes throughout the world, our residents and Sisters pray very specially for your intentions and for the needs of the Church. You will notice that we are very blessed to have our resident priests who contribute so much spiritually, not only to our home but also to the life of the Church through the joyful and faithful witness they give of their priesthood.

We recall with great happiness and deep

>

© www.papalvisit.org.uk

appreciation the canonisation of our Foundress, St Jeanne Jugan, in Rome, on the 11th October last year. Her message of love, respect and care of the elderly is more actual than ever in today's society. On that day, Holy Father, when referring to St Jeanne Jugan, you greatly encouraged us with these words:

"Her charism is ever timely while so many elderly people are suffering from numerous forms of poverty and solitude… May St Jeanne Jugan be for elderly people a living source of hope."

May we, her daughters, always cherish her charism and follow, with a spirit of love and generosity, in her footsteps.

Thank you, Holy Father, for showing us your loving concern for the elderly. Thank you from the bottom of our hearts for being here with us today. Your visit will always remain a source of immense joy and something we shall treasure for the rest of our lives! ■

Welcome Holy Father - Sr. Marie Claire Brennan.

Dear Holy Father,

All the residents here in St Peter's are tremendously honoured that you have chosen to come to us today. It is such a great privilege! Thank you for showing your care for us.

We always listen for your words of encouragement to the elderly all over the world. They are a great source of comfort and inspiration. ■

Holy Father we all love you.
Thank you and once again welcome -
Mrs Patricia Fasky.

Pope Benedict's speech to St Peter's residents and staff

St Peter's Residence, Vauxhall, Saturday 18th September 2010. 5:25pm

My dear Brothers and Sisters,

I am very pleased to be among you, the residents of St Peter's, and to thank Sr. Marie Claire and Mrs. Fasky for their kind words of welcome on your behalf. I am also pleased to greet Archbishop Smith of Southwark, as well as the Little Sisters of the Poor and the personnel and volunteers who look after you.

As advances in medicine and other factors lead to increased longevity, it is important to recognise the presence of growing numbers of older people as a blessing for society. Every generation can learn from the experience and wisdom of the generation that preceded it. Indeed the provision of care for the elderly should be considered not so much an act of generosity as the repayment of a debt of gratitude.

For her part, the Church has always had great respect for the elderly. The Fourth Commandment,

"Honour your father and your mother as the Lord your God commanded you" *(Deut 5:16),* is linked to the promise, "that your days may be prolonged, and that it may go well with you, in the land which the Lord your God gives you" *(Deut 5:16).* This work of the Church for the aging and infirm not only provides love and care for them, but is also rewarded by God with the blessings he promises on the land where this commandment is observed. God wills a proper respect for the dignity and worth, the health and well-being of the elderly and, through her charitable institutions in Britain and beyond, the Church seeks to fulfil the Lord's command to respect life, regardless of age or circumstances.

At the very start of my pontificate I said, "Each of us is willed, each of us is loved, each of us is necessary" *(Homily at the Mass for the Beginning of the Petrine* >

© PA Photos.

The tiny stage was decked with yellow and white flowers; in front of it stood a mosaic of St Peter, which the Pope gave to the home, and a gold chasuble, which the residents and nuns gave the Pope.

While the sisters and staff members energetically reached out to shake or kiss the Pope's hand, it was the Pope who approached many of the elderly, grasping their hands with both of his.

Pope Benedict also used his visit to St Peter's as an opportunity to reaffirm Church teaching about the value of human life at every stage of its development and to urge people to love and respect the elderly.

As human longevity increases in many countries, he said, people must learn to see the growing number of elderly as a blessing for society.

"Every generation can learn from the experience and wisdom of the generation that preceded it," he said, adding that care for older citizens is not a burden, but the repayment of a debt of gratitude.

Ministry of the Bishop of Rome, 24th April 2005). Life is a unique gift, at every stage from conception until natural death, and it is God's alone to give and to take. One may enjoy good health in old age; but equally Christians should not be afraid to share in the suffering of Christ, if God wills that we struggle with infirmity. My predecessor, the late Pope John Paul, suffered very publicly during the last years of his life. It was clear to all of us that he did so in union with the sufferings of our Saviour. His cheerfulness and forbearance as he faced his final days were a remarkable and moving example to all of us who have to carry the burden of advancing years.

In this sense, I come among you not only as a father, but also as a brother who knows well the joys and the struggles that come with age. Our long years of life afford us the opportunity to appreciate both the beauty of God's greatest gift to us, the gift of life, as well as the fragility of the human spirit. Those of us who live many years are given a marvellous chance to deepen our awareness of the mystery of Christ, who humbled himself to share in our humanity. As the normal span of our lives increases, our physical capacities are often diminished; and yet these times may well be among the most spiritually fruitful years of our lives. These years are an opportunity to remember in affectionate prayer all those whom we have cherished in this life, and to place all that we have personally been and done before the mercy and tenderness of God. This will surely be a great spiritual comfort and enable us to discover anew his love and goodness all the days of our life.

With these sentiments, dear brothers and sisters, I am pleased to assure you of my prayers for you all, and I ask for your prayers for me. May Our Blessed Lady and her spouse St Joseph intercede for our happiness in this life and obtain for us the blessing of a serene passage to the next.

May God bless you all! ■

Holy Father's address to safeguarding professionals

St Peter's Residence, Vauxhall, Saturday 18th September 2010. 5:45pm

Dear Friends,
I am glad to have the opportunity to greet you, who represent the many professionals and volunteers responsible for child protection in Church environments. The Church has a long tradition of caring for children from their earliest years through to adulthood, following the affectionate example of Christ, who blessed the children brought to him, and who taught his disciples that to such as these the Kingdom of Heaven belongs (cf. Mk 10:13-16).

Your work, carried out within the framework of the recommendations made in the first instance by the Nolan Report and subsequently by the Cumberlege Commission, has made a vital contribution to the promotion of safe environments for young people. It helps to ensure that the preventative measures put in place are effective, that they are maintained with vigilance, and that any allegations of abuse are dealt with swiftly and justly. On behalf of the many children you serve and their parents, let me thank you for the good work that you have done and continue to do in this field.

It is deplorable that, in such marked contrast to the Church's long tradition of care for them, children have suffered abuse and mistreatment at the hands of some priests and religious. We have all become much more aware of the need to safeguard children, and you are an important part of the Church's broad-ranging response to the problem. While there are never grounds for complacency, credit should be given where it is due: the efforts of the Church in this country and elsewhere, especially in the last ten years, to guarantee the safety of children and young people and to show them every respect as they grow to maturity, should be acknowledged. I pray that your generous service will help to reinforce an atmosphere of trust and renewed commitment to the welfare of children, who are such a precious gift from God.

May God prosper your work, and may he pour out his blessings upon all of you. ■

Streets fill with papal fans, with a bit of humour

Papal supporters tended to lean more toward cute than clever, several going so far as to decorate their bright yellow Wellington rain boots with "I love the Pope" messages. There also was the hand-drawn sign, "We love U papa more than beans on toast."

Niamh Maloney, who carried the sign to almost every event in London and Birmingham said, "We are unofficial members of the Pope's entourage. We've been walking for three days with these posters. I'm a papal stalker."

Maloney, a youth minister for the Diocese of Northhampton, and her group also had a sign that said, "Holiness is the only X factor." The youth minister said that after so many negative stories in the media before the papal trip, "we just wanted a bit of a laugh." ■ PICS: © PA Photos.

(left) Pope Benedict XVI makes his way down the Mall in London on his way to Hyde Park.

(far right) (From left to right) Amber-Louise Large, Christabel Lunghu and Josephine Clarke, all 12 and from Trowbridge, Wiltshire, in Hyde Park to attend a Prayer Vigil led by Pope Benedict XVI.
© PA Photos.

Holy Nation, Royal Priesthood

The music this afternoon in Hyde Park has been uplifting. Everyone is excited, joyful and singing their hearts out are the choir, who led the singing during the procession of tha banners. This was an amazing spectacle. The young people from each diocese led the procession, followed by representatives of parishes from up and down the land. Seeing so many people, in a procession that just went on and on, was fantastic.

Several great songs were sung during this time. Christ be our light, One bread one body, Shine Jesus shine, We are marching in the light of God and one, in particular that seemed to be exceptionally apt today, Out of darkness.

Out of darkness, God has called us,
claimed by Christ as God's own people.
Holy nation, royal priesthood,
walking in God's marv'lous light.

The crowd here are people who have come out of the darkness of the past into God's light, brought there by the visit of Pope Benedict. We are now a holy nation, this visit has shown the people of this land what a nation we are, and now we must go forward and work to build upon this great opportunity to be the royal priesthood of believers.

http://thepapalvisit.wordpress.com/

Archbishop Peter Smith welcomes the Holy Father to Hyde Park

Hyde Park, Saturday 18th September 2010. 7:05pm

Most Holy Father, we welcome you this evening: from the heart of London, from the hearts of all of us here in Hyde Park, and from the hearts of all those united with us in prayer on television, radio and the internet.

This afternoon, Holy Father, as we were preparing for your arrival, we reflected prayerfully on how the Catholic Church plays its part in harnessing the spirit of humble and loving service through the work of its agencies and charities at home and abroad. As a Catholic community we know that authentic Christian life must be grounded in a daily spiritual encounter with the living God, and in fulfilling the command of Jesus Christ, "Love one another as I have loved you."

We have come from all over Britain to share this historic moment with you, and to celebrate and rejoice in the truth that God loves every human being unconditionally, irrespective of race, colour or creed. With you this evening we witness to the joy of being a follower of Jesus Christ, the light of the world, who stands at the door of every heart patiently waiting to be let in.

Holy Father, where we stand has a profound historical significance. Over 400 years ago Catholic and Anglican martyrs witnessed to their faith in Jesus Christ when they were put to death at Tyburn, a short distance from here. We give thanks to God that in more recent times, the Christian Churches in our land work together in the light of the Gospel for the common good of all in this country.

There is so much that unites us and we are committed to continuing the search for that visible unity for which Christ prayed.

During our liturgy this evening, on the eve of the beatification of Cardinal John Henry Newman, we will spend time in Christ's presence, meditating on the scriptures and on Cardinal Newman's life and words. We pray that our hearts will be ever more open to the presence and power of the Holy Spirit so that our lives may radiate the Light of Christ to those around us.

Finally, Holy Father, we assure you of our love, our support and our prayers; for your ministry as Chief Shepherd of the Church; for coming to confirm us in the faith; and especially for teaching us by your own example what it means to be steadfast in our fidelity to the person and teaching of Jesus Christ. Thank you, Holy Father, for being with us this evening and for leading us now in this Vigil of Prayer. ■

The Holy Father's Hyde Park Vigil address

Hyde Park, Saturday 18th September 2010. 8:30pm

My Brothers and Sisters in Christ,

This is an evening of joy, of immense spiritual joy, for all of us. We are gathered here in prayerful vigil to prepare for tomorrow's Mass, during which a great son of this nation, Cardinal John Henry Newman, will be declared Blessed. How many people, in England and throughout the world, have longed for this moment! It is also a great joy for me, personally, to share this experience with you. As you know, Newman has long been an important influence in my own life and thought, as he has been for so many people beyond these isles. The drama of Newman's life invites us to examine our lives, to see them against the vast horizon of God's plan, and to grow in communion with the Church of every time and place: the Church of the apostles, the Church of the martyrs, the Church of the saints, the Church which Newman loved and to whose mission he devoted his entire life.

I thank Archbishop Peter Smith for his kind words of welcome in your name, and I am especially pleased to see the many young people who are present for this vigil. This evening, in the context of our common prayer, I would like to reflect with you about a few aspects of Newman's life which I consider very relevant to our lives as believers and to the life of the Church today.

Let me begin by recalling that Newman, by his own account, traced the course of his whole life back to a powerful experience of conversion which he had as a young man. It was an immediate experience of the truth of God's word, of the objective reality of Christian revelation as handed down in the Church. This

>

experience, at once religious and intellectual, would inspire his vocation to be a minister of the Gospel, his discernment of the source of authoritative teaching in the Church of God, and his zeal for the renewal of ecclesial life in fidelity to the apostolic tradition. At the end of his life, Newman would describe his life's work as a struggle against the growing tendency to view religion as a purely private and subjective matter, a question of personal opinion. Here is the first lesson we can learn from his life: in our day, when an intellectual and moral relativism threatens to sap the very foundations of our society, Newman reminds us that, as men and women made in the image and likeness of God, we were created to know the truth, to find in that truth our ultimate freedom and the fulfilment of our deepest human aspirations. In a word, we are meant to know Christ, who is himself "the way, and the truth, and the life" *(Jn 14:6)*.

Newman's life also teaches us that passion for the truth, intellectual honesty and genuine conversion are costly. The truth that sets us free cannot be kept to ourselves; it calls for testimony, it begs to be heard, and in the end its convincing power comes from itself and not from the human eloquence or arguments in which it may be couched. Not far from here, at Tyburn, great numbers of our brothers and sisters died for the faith; the witness of their fidelity to the end was ever more powerful than the inspired words that so many of them spoke before surrendering everything to the Lord. In our own time, the price to be paid for fidelity to the Gospel is no longer being hanged, drawn and quartered but it often involves being dismissed out of hand, ridiculed or parodied. And yet, the Church cannot withdraw from the task of proclaiming Christ and his Gospel as saving truth, the source of our ultimate happiness as individuals and as the foundation of a just and humane society.

Finally, Newman teaches us that if we have accepted the truth of Christ and committed our lives to him, there can be no separation between what we believe and the way we live our lives. Our every thought, word and action must be directed to the glory of God and the

(right) Former Archbishop of Westminster Cardinal Cormac Murphy O'Connor (left) and current Archbishop of Westminster Vincent Nichols (second left) watch as Pope Benedict XVI leads a Prayer Vigil at Hyde Park, London. © PA Photos.

The service at Hyde Park was preceded by film clips on social and human rights issues, as well as hymns from South Africa and Cameroon and performances by Polish, Roma and English dance and theatre groups.

A prison pastor, former heroin addict and parents of a murdered teenager also spoke before the Pope's arrival. As he entered the park, musicians performed George Frideric Handel's *Messiah* and Antonio Vivaldi's *Gloria*.

Rachel Moran, a student from Lincoln, who came to the vigil with her face painted in the white and yellow of the Vatican flag, said: "It's a real challenge to be a young Christian today, but the Pope's visit has at least given us a chance to make noise and use our energy."

"It isn't true that young people are not interested and don't believe. They just need encouragement and very often don't get it," she added.

Irish singing trio, The Priests, performed during the service, and soprano Liam McNally, a 14-year-old contestant on the popular TV programme *Britain's Got Talent,* sang the Our Father. ∎

© Catholic News Service.

spread of his Kingdom. Newman understood this, and was the great champion of the prophetic office of the Christian laity. He saw clearly that we do not so much accept the truth in a purely intellectual act as embrace it in a spiritual dynamic that penetrates to the core of our being. Truth is passed on not merely by formal teaching, important as that is, but also by the witness of lives lived in integrity, fidelity and holiness; those who live in and by the truth instinctively recognise what is false and, precisely as false, inimical to the beauty and goodness which accompany the splendour of truth, *veritatis splendor.*

Tonight's first reading is the magnificent prayer in which St Paul asks that we be granted to know "the love of Christ which surpasses all understanding" *(Eph 3:14-21).* The Apostle prays that Christ may dwell in our hearts through faith *(cf. Eph 3:17)* and that we may come to "grasp, with all the saints, the breadth and the length, the height and the depth" of that love. Through faith we come to see God's word as a lamp for our steps and light for our path *(cf. Ps 119:105).* Newman, like the countless saints who preceded him along the path of Christian discipleship, taught that the "kindly light" of faith leads us to realize the truth about ourselves, our dignity as God's children, and the sublime destiny

which awaits us in heaven. By letting the light of faith shine in our hearts, and by abiding in that light through our daily union with the Lord in prayer and participation in the life-giving sacraments of the Church, we ourselves become light to those around us; we exercise our "prophetic office"; often, without even knowing it, we draw people one step closer to the Lord and his truth. Without the life of prayer, without the interior transformation which takes place through the grace of the sacraments, we cannot, in Newman's words, "radiate Christ"; we become just another "clashing cymbal" *(1 Cor 13:1)* in a world filled with growing noise and confusion, filled with false paths leading only to heartbreak and illusion.

One of the Cardinal's best-loved meditations includes the words, "God has created me to do him some definite service. He has committed some work to me which he has not committed to another" *(Meditations on Christian Doctrine).* Here we see Newman's fine Christian realism, the point at which faith and life inevitably intersect. Faith is meant to bear fruit in the transformation of our world through the power of the Holy Spirit at work in the lives and activity of believers. No one who looks realistically at our world today could think that Christians can afford to go on with business as usual, ignoring the profound crisis of faith which has >

overtaken our society, or simply trusting that the patrimony of values handed down by the Christian centuries will continue to inspire and shape the future of our society. We know that in times of crisis and upheaval God has raised up great saints and prophets for the renewal of the Church and Christian society; we trust in his providence and we pray for his continued guidance. But each of us, in accordance with his or her state of life, is called to work for the advancement of God's Kingdom by imbuing temporal life with the values of the Gospel. Each of us has a mission, each of us is called to change the world, to work for a culture of life, a culture forged by love and respect for the dignity of each human person. As our Lord tells us in the Gospel we have just heard, our light must shine in the sight of all, so that, seeing our good works, they may give praise to our heavenly Father *(cf. Mt 5:16)*.

Here I wish to say a special word to the many young people present. Dear young friends: only Jesus knows what "definite service" he has in mind for you. Be open to his voice resounding in the depths of your heart: even now his heart is speaking to your heart. Christ has need of families to remind the world of the dignity of human love and the beauty of family life. He needs men and women who devote their lives to the noble task of education, tending the young and forming them in the ways of the Gospel. He needs those who will consecrate their lives to the pursuit of perfect charity, following him in chastity, poverty and obedience, and serving him in the least of our brothers and sisters. He needs the powerful love of contemplative religious, who sustain the Church's witness and activity through their constant prayer. And he needs priests, good and holy priests, men who are willing to lay down their lives for their sheep. Ask Our Lord what he has in mind for you! Ask him for the generosity to say "yes!" Do not be afraid to give yourself totally to Jesus. He will give you the grace you need to fulfil your vocation. Let me finish these few words by warmly inviting you to join me next year in Madrid for World Youth Day. It is always a wonderful occasion to grow in love for Christ and to be encouraged in a joyful life of faith along with thousands of other young people. I hope to see many of you there!

And now, dear friends, let us continue our vigil of prayer by preparing to encounter Christ, present among us in the Blessed Sacrament of the Altar. Together, in the silence of our common adoration, let us open our minds and hearts to his presence, his love, and the convincing power of his truth. In a special way, let us thank him for the enduring witness to that truth offered by Cardinal John Henry Newman. Trusting in his prayers, let us ask the Lord to illumine our path, and the path of all British society, with the kindly light of his truth, his love and his peace. Amen. ∎

Pope Benedict XVI leads a prayer vigil at Hyde Park, London. Tens of thousands of people gathered for the service on the eve of the beatification of Cardinal John Henry Newman. © Catholic News Service.

Tyburn
Triangular Gateway to Life

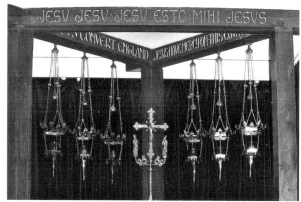

Replica of Tyburn Gallows in the Shrine of the Marytrs, Tyburn Convent

A faint whisper came from the man in the now bloodied white habit as the executioner roughly pulled his beating heart up out of his body: "Good Jesu, what will you do with my heart?"

He was John Houghton: Essex born, and educated at Cambridge; Canon and Civil lawyer; Parish priest, Carthusian Prior– and proto-martyr. It was the morning of May 4, 1535 at Tyburn Gallows outside the City of London. With him that day were two other Carthusian Priors – Augustine Webster and Robert Lawrence; Richard Reynolds a Brigettine priest of Syon Abbey, and John Haile, secular priest.

Their crime was the refusal to take the Oath of Supremacy which declared that King Henry VIII was the Supreme Head of the Church in England. This refusal was thereafter deemed to be high treason.

The five had been brought out from their various prison cells in the Tower of London and tied to hurdles- low wooden frames – on which they were to be dragged the three miles to Tyburn. Looking out his window, St. Thomas More said to his daughter Margaret, "Lo, dost thou not see, Meg, that these blessed Fathers be now going to their deaths as gladly as a bridegroom going to a marriage feast?"

For many long years Tyburn had been the king's gallows for London and Middlesex. William FitzOsbert's execution in 1196 was the first to be recorded. Now, for 150 years, Tyburn - a place of cruelty, torture and execution, became a place where people suffered for their religious belief.

Religious and secular priests, brothers, laymen and laywomen followed one another courageously onto the gallows until Oliver Plunket, Archbishop of Armagh and Primate of all Ireland became the 105th - and final – martyr on 11 July 1681.

Today, just 300 yards from the known site of the gallows, the Shrine of the Sacred Heart and the Tyburn Martyrs honours not only those who won the palm of martyrdom here, but all 305 English and Welsh reformation martyrs. The newly completed access work means that pilgrims, tourists, school groups and visitors all now have easy access to both the Chapel and the Crypt Shrine.

A Sister is available for GUIDED TOURS of the Shrine daily at 10.30 a.m., 3.30pm and 5.30pm.

The MONASTIC AFTERNOONS are on the first Sunday of every month 2.30pm - 5.00pm. Everyone is invited to listen to a talk on the Martyrs, share a cup of tea, discover more about Benedictine life in a second talk, and then join the community for the singing of Vespers.

HOLY MASS is celebrated at 7.30am every day of the year. Exposition of the Holy Eucharist continues all day and all night. The Church is open to the public from 6.30am to 8.30pm daily.

The keepers of the Shrine are the Benedictine Adorers of the Sacred Heart of Jesus of Montmartre, known all around the world as **"The Tyburn Nuns". Tyburn Convent, 8 Hyde Park Place, London. W2 2LJ. Telephone 020 7723 7262.**

Already We Hold You In Prayer

Living in the heart of London, the Tyburn Benedictine Community has as its special mission, prayer for the people of England and Wales. Our monastery is built on the site of the Tyburn gallows where 105 Catholics were martyred during the reformation. Our life of prayer draws Sisters from many nations.

If you have a special intention, let us know and we will remember it specifically in our prayer. You may like to use the space below.

☐ Yes, please remember my intention/s in prayer.

....
....
....

☐ Yes, please send me the free booklet on the Tyburn Martyrs
☐ Yes I'm interested – please send me vocations details.
☐ I'd like to become a founding donor of your new Monastery in Hamilton, New Zealand. My gift of £ .... is enclosed payable to **Tyburn Convent.**

Name: ....
Address: ....
....
....Please print

(photocopies accepted)

RETURN TO: Mother General,
Tyburn Convent, 8 Hyde Park Place,
London. W2 2LJ. Tel: 020 7723 7262

Mary and Joseph

BLESSED JOHN HENRY NEWMAN

SUNDAY 19TH SEPTEMBER 2010
FEAST DAY 9TH OCTOBER

I met Mary on the footpath this morning, as we were walking from the coach park to Cofton Park. Originally from Kerala, South India, she came today with her parish, St Michael's in Shepton Mallet. They left there at 4am, and she had been up since 2am. She was pushing her husband, Joseph, in a wheelchair. Another pilgrim noticed her struggling a bit when the path sloped and offered to help her push. After a while I took a turn, and ended up staying with them right into the wheelchair enclosure.

The rain was falling steadily by now and Mary said it was a blessing. I wondered at first what she meant, but then I realised that in her homeland that is exactly what rain is, a blessing from God. Of course this rain was nothing like monsoon rain. In fact, Mary told me, it doesn't actually rain at all in England. She also said that the more we suffered on this pilgrimage, the greater would be the blessings we received. She was praying for a miracle to help her husband to walk again.

As we drew nearer to the entrance a queue formed. The ground was undulating and muddy and the temporary metal paths put down to get us across the bumps were still rather difficult to negotiate with a wheechair. An angel appeared in the form of a policewoman who patiently explained to me how to sort out the brakes on this wheelchair, which was of a kind unfamiliar to me. She also guided us through a grassy area, recommending going backwards in order to stop slipping. I thanked her, and said how good it was that she had received wheelchair training. She said it was not her training, but her mum, who uses a wheelchair, that had given her those skills. God has a way of putting people in the right place at the right time.

I must admit to feeling a little frustrated that even using the wheelchair entrance we had to queue. The walking pilgrims were on the wheelchair path as well, and there was no way we got priority. As a veteran of Lourdes I felt things could have been better organised, but Mary reminded me that we need to suffer a little for our faith.

Once I had said my goodbyes to Mary and Joseph in the wheelchair enclosure I tried to make my way to the media centre. This was easier said than done, and the first dozen or so stewards who I asked didn't have a clue there was a media centre. My spirits sank for a while, as one of my shoes had started to leak and I wondered if I would ever find the media centre. Fortunately I heard the familiar sound of Jo Boyce and Mike Stanley singing *Bread of Life* and I started to feel better. Even more uplifting was Jo singing her setting of the *Magnificat.*

Eventually after one or two false starts and diversions, I found the entrance gate which I should have entered, and there, to my amazement, was someone I had met on a pilgrimage to Iona, four years ago. At last there was someone who could tell me where the media centre was. The VAMPs (Vatican Accredited Media Persons) had not yet arrived, so there was still plenty of space for me to set up the laptop and get to work with my story.

Suddenly I noticed that the sun had come out, the Pope had landed, the choir were singing, and a faint rainbow could be seen over Crofton Park. My

view of the popemobile was the best I've had so far.

Church of God, elect and glorious,
holy nation, chosen race;
called as God's own special people,
royal priests and heirs of grace;
know the purpose of your calling,
show to all his mighty deeds;
tell of love which knows no limits,
grace which meets all human needs.

http://thepapalvisit.wordpress.com/

Archbishop Longley's Cofton Park welcome to the Holy Father

Cofton Park, Birmingham, Sunday 19th September 2010. 10:25am

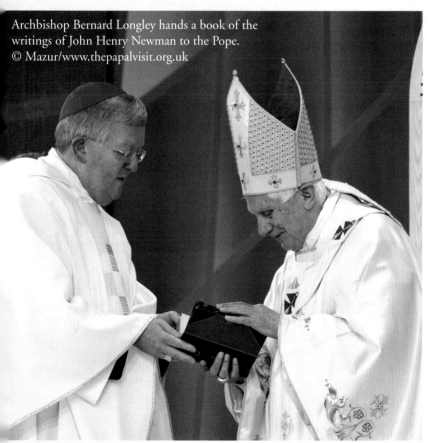

Archbishop Bernard Longley hands a book of the writings of John Henry Newman to the Pope.
© Mazur/www.thepapalvisit.org.uk

Most Holy Father,
It is with great joy that I welcome you here to Birmingham on the final morning of your visit. Over recent days you have been among us as a pilgrim sharing your own search for the truth and goodness of God. As our Supreme Pastor you have led us closer to Jesus Christ to be refreshed from the

"well-springs of the Trinity".

In following your Apostolic journey we have seen you reach out and touch the hearts and minds of many, within our countries and beyond, by being in our midst and by making us more aware of the presence of Christ the Good Shepherd. As the Successor of Peter you have encouraged us to draw closer to the rock upon which the Church is built and to recognise it as the true source of living water that can quench our thirst.

Now, Holy Father, we are united with you in prayer in this city which was the chosen and adopted home of the Venerable John Henry Newman. We gather close to the place where his earthly remains were laid to rest and in these hills where he would often come for refreshment and peace. In this place we thank you for presenting him to us anew – a sure well-spring of goodness and truth where we may find refreshment and strength for our own pilgrimage of faith.

As we come to celebrate his beatification with you today we give thanks to God for all those whose influence brought blessings to Cardinal Newman - especially for those who had nurtured his faith within the Church of England and for Blessed Dominic of the Mother of God who first ministered to him sacramentally within the Catholic Church.

We ask you, Holy Father, to draw us again into the Eucharistic presence of the Lord so that we may soon acclaim the Venerable John Henry Newman among the Blessed. ∎

Pope Benedict's Beatification Homily

Cofton Park, Birmingham, Sunday 19th September 2010. 11:15am

Dear Brothers and Sisters in Christ,

This day that has brought us together here in Birmingham is a most auspicious one. In the first place, it is the Lord's day, Sunday, the day when our Lord Jesus Christ rose from the dead and changed the course of human history for ever, offering new life and hope to all who live in darkness and in the shadow of death. That is why Christians all over the world come together on this day to give praise and thanks to God for the great marvels he has worked for us. This particular Sunday also marks a significant moment in the life of the British nation, as it is the day chosen to commemorate the 70th anniversary of the Battle of Britain. For me as one who lived and suffered through the dark days of

the Nazi regime in Germany, it is deeply moving to be here with you on this occasion, and to recall how many of your fellow citizens sacrificed their lives, courageously resisting the forces of that evil ideology. My thoughts go in particular to nearby Coventry, which suffered such heavy bombardment and massive loss of life in November 1940. Seventy years later, we recall with shame and horror the dreadful toll of death and destruction that war brings in its wake, and we renew our resolve to work for peace and reconciliation wherever the threat of conflict looms. Yet there is another, more joyful reason why this is an auspicious day for Great Britain, for the Midlands, for Birmingham. It is the day that sees Cardinal John Henry Newman formally   >

Pope Benedict XVI next to a relic of John Henry Newman.
© Mazur/www.thepapalvisit.org.uk

Pilgrims were required to arrive at the Mass site hours before the Pope, so they waited in a drizzle huddled in the dark with hands wrapped around steaming thermos cups of tea.

Katrina and Steve Herbert arrived from Aldershot shortly after 4am with their eight children, ages 13 years to 13 months.

"We have frozen. The kids have been pale green most of the day," the mum said, but "it's wonderful to be here. It's an incredible day for our country and for Catholics."

The bishops' official papal visit Twitter feed said: "A true English beatification: cold, wet, rainy."

Ian Johnston, 50, who came to Birmingham with an Irish group from the Neocatechumenal Way, said, "It was wonderful to see the sun come out as soon as the Pope arrived." ■

raised to the altars and declared Blessed.

I thank Archbishop Bernard Longley for his gracious welcome at the start of Mass this morning. I pay tribute to all who have worked so hard over many years to promote the cause of Cardinal Newman, including the Fathers of the Birmingham Oratory and the members of the Spiritual Family Das Werk. And I greet everyone here from Great Britain, Ireland, and further afield; I thank you for your presence at this celebration, in which we give glory and praise to God for the heroic virtue of a saintly Englishman.

England has a long tradition of martyr saints, whose courageous witness has sustained and inspired the Catholic community here for centuries. Yet it is right and fitting that we should recognise today the holiness of a confessor, a son of this nation who, while not called to shed his blood for the Lord, nevertheless bore eloquent witness to him in the course of a long >

Pope Benedict XVI hands over the Book of Gospels to Deacon Jack Sullivan.
© Mazur/www.thepapalvisit.org.uk

life devoted to the priestly ministry, and especially to preaching, teaching, and writing. He is worthy to take his place in a long line of saints and scholars from these islands, St Bede, St Hilda, St Aelred, Blessed Duns Scotus, to name but a few. In Blessed John Henry, that tradition of gentle scholarship, deep human wisdom and profound love for the Lord has borne rich fruit, as a sign of the abiding presence of the Holy Spirit deep within the heart of God's people, bringing forth abundant gifts of holiness.

Cardinal Newman's motto, **Cor ad cor loquitur, or 'Heart speaks unto heart',** gives us an insight into his understanding of the Christian life as a call to holiness, experienced as the profound desire of the human heart to enter into intimate communion with the Heart of God. He reminds us that faithfulness to prayer gradually transforms us into the divine likeness. As he wrote in one of his many fine sermons, "a habit of prayer, the practice of turning to God and the unseen world in every season, in every place, in every emergency – prayer, I say, has what may be called a natural effect in spiritualising and elevating the soul. A man is no longer what he was before; gradually … he has imbibed a new set of ideas, and become imbued with fresh principles" *(Parochial and Plain Sermons, iv, 230-231).* Today's Gospel tells us that no one can be the servant of two

Pope Benedict XVI leads Mass and the beatification of Cardinal John Henry Newman at Cofton Park in Birmingham. Blessed John Henry Newman, a 19th-century theologian and a prolific writer on spiritual topics, left the Anglican Church and embraced Catholicism at the age of 44.
© Catholic News Service.

masters *(cf. Lk 16:13),* and Blessed John Henry's teaching on prayer explains how the faithful Christian is definitively taken into the service of the one true Master, who alone has a claim to our unconditional devotion *(cf. Mt 23:10).* Newman helps us to understand what this means for our daily lives: he tells us that our divine Master has assigned a specific task to each one of us, a "definite service", committed uniquely to every single person: "I have my mission", he wrote, "I am a link in a chain, a bond of connexion between persons. He has not created me for naught. I shall do good, I shall do his work; I shall be ⟩

A giant portrait of Blessed John Henry Newman hangs behind the altar, and smaller likenesses were carried to the Mass by many of the faithful who filled Cofton Park.

Pope Benedict and the main concelebrants of the Mass processed to the altar while the choir and crowd sang *Praise to the Holiest in the Height,* a hymn with lyrics written by Cardinal Newman. The lyrics to the offertory hymn *Firmly I Believe and Truly,* also were written by the cardinal.

The Pope announced that his feast day would be the 9th October, the day of his entry into the Catholic Church, but he did not mention his conversion or his relationship with Anglicanism.

But welcoming Pope Benedict, Archbishop Bernard Longley of Birmingham offered a prayer of thanks for the Anglicans who nurtured Cardinal Newman's faith and for Blessed Dominic Barberi, a Passionist priest who welcomed him into the Catholic Church in 1845.

Deacon Jack Sullivan, whose healing from a crippling spinal condition in August 2001 was the miracle that allowed for Cardinal Newman's beatification, read the Gospel at the Mass. Earlier in the liturgy, after the Pope read the decree of beatification, Deacon Sullivan and his wife, Carol, carried a relic of Blessed John Henry Newman to Pope Benedict.

He is worthy to take his place in a long line of saints and scholars from these islands, St Bede, St Hilda, St Aelred, Blessed Duns Scotus, to name but a few. In Blessed John Henry, that tradition of gentle scholarship, deep human wisdom and profound love for the Lord has borne rich fruit, as a sign of the abiding presence of the Holy Spirit deep within the heart of God's people, bringing forth abundant gifts of holiness.

an angel of peace, a preacher of truth in my own place … if I do but keep his commandments and serve him in my calling" *(Meditations and Devotions, 301-2).*

The definite service to which Blessed John Henry was called involved applying his keen intellect and his prolific pen to many of the most pressing "subjects of the day". His insights into the relationship between faith and reason, into the vital place of revealed religion in civilised society, and into the need for a broadly-based and wide-ranging

approach to education were not only of profound importance for Victorian England, but continue today to inspire and enlighten many all over the world. I would like to pay particular tribute to his vision for education, which has done so much to shape the ethos that is the driving force behind Catholic schools and colleges today. Firmly opposed to any reductive or utilitarian approach, he sought to achieve an educational environment in which intellectual training, moral discipline and religious commitment would come together. The project to found a Catholic University in Ireland provided him with an opportunity to develop his ideas on the

The congregation listens to Pope Benedict XVI during the Mass to beatify Cardinal John Henry Newman at Cofton Park. © PA Photos.

subject, and the collection of discourses that he published as *The Idea of a University* holds up an ideal from which all those engaged in academic formation can continue to learn. And indeed, what better goal could teachers of religion set themselves than Blessed John Henry's famous appeal for an intelligent, well-instructed laity: "I want a laity, not arrogant, not rash in speech, not disputatious, but men who know their religion, who enter into it, who know just where they stand, who know what they hold and what they do not, who know their creed so well that they can give an account of it, who know so much of history that they can defend it" *(The Present Position of Catholics in England, ix, 390).* On this day when the author of those words is raised to the altars, I pray that, through his intercession and example, all who are engaged in the task of teaching and catechesis will be inspired to greater effort by the vision he so clearly sets before us.

While it is John Henry Newman's intellectual legacy that has understandably received most attention in the vast literature devoted to his life and work, I prefer on this occasion to conclude with a brief reflection on his life as a priest, a pastor of souls. The warmth and humanity underlying his appreciation of the pastoral ministry is beautifully expressed in another of his famous sermons: "Had Angels been your priests, my brethren, they could not have condoled with you, sympathised with you, have had compassion on you, felt tenderly for you, and made allowances for you, as we can; they could not have been your patterns and guides, and have led you on from your old selves into a new life, as they can who come from the midst of you" *("Men, not Angels: the Priests of the Gospel", Discourses to Mixed Congregations, 3).* He lived out that profoundly human vision of priestly ministry in his devoted care for the people of Birmingham during the years that he spent at the Oratory he founded, visiting the sick and the poor, comforting the bereaved, caring for those in prison. No wonder that on his death so many thousands of people lined the local streets as his body was taken to its place of burial not half a mile from here. One hundred and twenty years later, great crowds have assembled once again to rejoice in the Church's solemn recognition of the outstanding holiness of this much-loved father of souls. What better way to express the joy of this moment than by turning to our heavenly Father in heartfelt thanksgiving, praying in the words that Blessed John Henry Newman placed on the lips of the choirs of angels in heaven:

Praise to the Holiest in the height
And in the depth be praise;
In all his words most wonderful,
Most sure in all his ways!
(The Dream of Gerontius). ■

Recitation of the Angelus Domini

Cofton Park, Birmingham, Sunday 19th September 2010. 12:00pm

Brothers and Sisters in Jesus Christ,
I am pleased to send my greetings to the people of Seville where, just yesterday, Madre María de la Purísima de la Cruz was beatified. May Blessed María be an inspiration to young women to follow her example of single-minded love of God and neighbour.

When Blessed John Henry Newman came to live in Birmingham, he gave the name 'Maryvale' to his first home here. The Oratory that he founded is dedicated to the Immaculate Conception of the Blessed Virgin. And the Catholic University of Ireland he placed under the patronage of Mary, Sedes Sapientiae. In so many ways, he lived his priestly ministry in a spirit of filial devotion to the Mother of God. Meditating upon her role in the unfolding of God's plan for our salvation, he was moved to exclaim: "Who can estimate the holiness and perfection of her, who was chosen to be the Mother of Christ? What must have been her gifts, who was chosen to be the only near earthly relative of the Son of God, the only one whom He was bound by nature to revere and look up to; the one appointed to train and educate Him, to instruct Him day by day, as He grew in wisdom and in stature?" (Parochial and Plain Sermons, ii, 131-2). It is on account of those abundant gifts of grace that we honour her, and it is on account of that intimacy with her divine Son that we naturally seek her intercession for our own needs and the needs of the whole world. In the words of the Angelus, we turn now to our Blessed Mother and commend to her the intentions that we hold in our hearts. ■

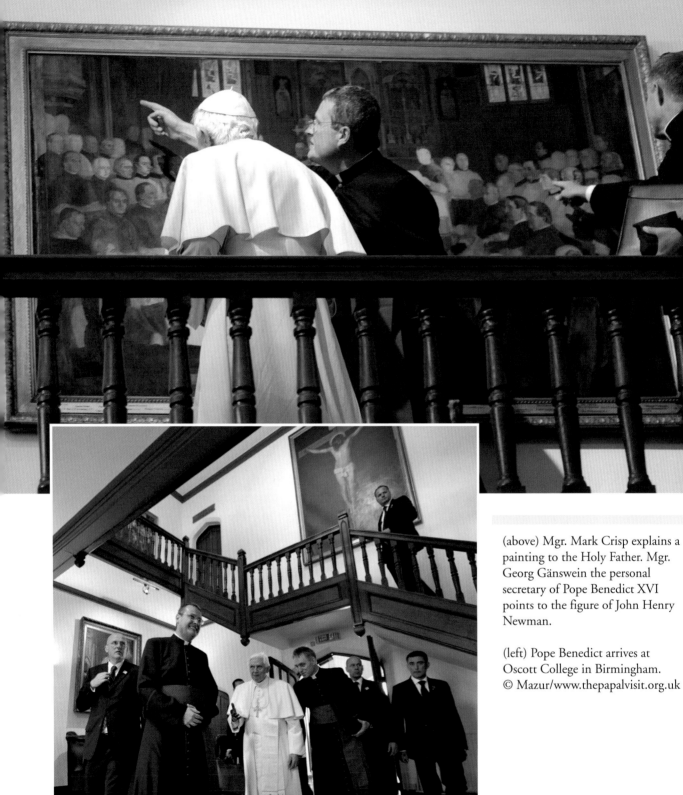

(above) Mgr. Mark Crisp explains a painting to the Holy Father. Mgr. Georg Gänswein the personal secretary of Pope Benedict XVI points to the figure of John Henry Newman.

(left) Pope Benedict arrives at Oscott College in Birmingham.
© Mazur/www.thepapalvisit.org.uk

Cardinal O'Brien's farewell address to Pope Benedict XVI

Oscott College, Birmingham, Sunday 19th September 2010. 5:20pm

Holy Father, it is a great privilege for me to address you, as Archbishop of St Andrews and Edinburgh and President of the Bishops' Conference of Scotland.

As you prepare to leave us, we remember the joy and pride we felt when we learned of your State visit to the United Kingdom at the invitation of Her Majesty the Queen and Her Government.

In Edinburgh, just three days ago, in the Palace of Holyroodhouse, Her Majesty, the Duke of Edinburgh and leaders of Church and State welcomed you and listened to the words you so thoughtfully delivered to us when you addressed our country.

It was a particular joy for us in Scotland to realise that you would arrive in our country to begin your visit on the 16th of September, the Feast of St Ninian. Ninian was of course a bishop, ordained in Rome and sent back to his homeland to spread the Christian message. Your words and your very presence brought to our minds our ancient Christian heritage.

The welcoming cavalcade along Princes Street in Edinburgh reminded a worldwide audience of the Christian roots of our land. Like Ninian before you, you too moved across our countries, strengthening us in that same Christian faith whose seed had been first sown over 1600 years ago.

At Bellahouston Park in Glasgow, the first of your Masses in our country was celebrated with great joy. For many months our people had been preparing to greet you with very great happiness in prayer and song. Major events followed in England, both temporal and spiritual, allowing you to engage with our fellow Catholics, our Christian brothers and sisters, with civil society, and all people of goodwill.

At the heart of your pilgrimage was the beatification of John Henry Cardinal Newman. We are happy to acknowledge the Scottish links of the new Blessed John Henry Newman – coming to Abbotsford in the Scottish Borders for relaxation and prayer and celebrating Mass on the occasions of his visits wearing the vestments which had been brought to my chapel in Edinburgh for you to see as a reminder of these Scottish links.

From your first encyclical letter *Deus Caritas Est,* your words have always been given detailed attention and careful study not only by the Catholic faithful but by peoples of all faiths and none.

As the chief teacher of our Faith we thank you for the guidance and inspiration you offer us. Your words to us; at Bellahouston Park, Twickenham, Westminster, Hyde Park, at the Beatification, and here in Birmingham will be studied and used to fortify us all in the faith passed on to us through the ages by the apostles and delivered over these four great days by the successor of Peter himself.

Your visit to us was both State and pastoral but our farewell to you is entirely personal. We thank you on behalf of all the people of the United Kingdom for agreeing to spend this time in our midst. On behalf of the bishops and priests gathered here and the whole people of God in our country, I pledge our love and fidelity to you and in asking for your prayers we offer the promise of our own prayers in the certain hope that Almighty God may indeed bless you, Holy Father, and inspire you in your service of love. ■

© PA Photos.

Archbishop Nichols' farewell speech to the Pope. In the background is the gift to the College of a beautiful mosaic of Mary presented by the Holy Father. © Mazur/www.thepapalvisit.org.uk

Archbishop Nichols' farewell address to Pope Benedict XVI

Oscott College, Birmingham, Sunday 19th September 2010. 5:30pm

Most Holy Father,

As we gather with you, together with our much loved Apostolic Nuncio, it is my joy and privilege to address you.

After all the joy, excitement and intensity of these four days of your most historic visit, we now cherish these moments of prayerful reflection with you.

This chapel holds a precious place in our history. It was here, in the first gathering of the newly appointed bishops, in 1852, that a new strategy for the Church in these countries was fashioned, a strategy which has proved to be enduring and fruitful. It centred on the importance of education in the faith and on the building up of parish life.

During the synod, the imagination of the bishops was fired by the powerful preaching of Fr. John Henry Newman, from that very pulpit. He was bold enough to speak of a new spring in the history of the Catholic faith in this place.

That historic moment has some resonances for us gathered here today. This moment with you is in a kind of 'Upper Room'. Here, in your guidance and blessing, we seek the inspiration of the Holy Spirit for our mission.

Time and again, you have spoken of the importance of the contribution of the Christian faith in our society, not least because, in your own words, 'if the moral principles underpinning the democratic process are themselves determined by nothing more solid than social consensus, then the fragility of the process becomes all too evident.'(Westminster Hall) We can already sense a new openness to this question, and to the role of faith communities, not only in the stance of the ⟩

Government but also in the hearts and willingness of so many people. We will pursue and build on these opportunities for the common good of all.

In speaking to us you have urged young people to find their fulfilment in a love for Christ, a love which will show them that, first, they are loved by Him. That must be true for us too. You have urged our priests to be faithful to their ministry and we bishops to be fathers to our priests. This we will strive to do. You have meditated with us on the 'unity between Christ's sacrifice on the Cross, the Eucharistic sacrifice which he has given to his Church and his eternal priesthood' in which we participate in daily living. Your words point to our baptismal calling 'to bring the reconciling power of his sacrifice to the world in which we live.'(Westminster Cathedral)

In this context, you have encouraged us in our work of safeguarding and shown an open heart to those who have suffered through our neglect. For this we thank you. You have reminded us of the importance of sensitive care of the elderly, offered with deep respect and recognition of their spiritual journey. You have reached out to our friends in other faiths, committing us again to work with them and seeking from them an open and reciprocal dialogue. You have led us in prayer and dialogue with our fellow brothers and sisters in Christ, strengthening our friendship and cooperation with them. The warmth and depth of our prayer together in Westminster Abbey will long remain in our hearts.

Holy Father, you give us new hearts for the tasks ahead, especially in the wonderful gift of declaring John Henry Newman as a blessed model for us to follow. It is an English parish priest whom you have beatified and this, for us, is the finest culmination of the Year for Priests. And, as we gather in this College chapel we recognise the importance of the work of fostering vocations and forming men to be the future generations of priests in these countries. This is a work to which we are deeply committed and I know you will give great joy to our seminarians when you greet them this afternoon before leaving.

Holy Father, in this visit you are contributing richly to our history and to the shaping of our future. You lift our hearts and reinvigorate us for our ministry especially in the example you give to us with your openness of heart, keenness of mind and gentle eloquence of expression in your unfailing witness to the mystery of Christ.

We take to heart your words that 'we need witnesses of the beauty of holiness, witnesses of the splendour of truth, witnesses of the joy and freedom born of a living relationship with Christ!' (Westminster Cathedral) This is our calling and we renew our dedication to it today.

Your visit to us was both State and pastoral but our farewell to you is entirely personal.

And so, Holy Father, we thank you on behalf of all the people of the United Kingdom for agreeing to spend this time in our midst. On behalf of the bishops and priests and the whole people of God in our country, I pledge our love and prayers for your vital and rich ministry in the Church and in the world. May Almighty God bless you, Holy Father, and inspire you in your service of love.

We also wish to thank you for the gift to this College of the beautiful mosaic of Mary and the child Jesus. It will be treasured.

And I would now ask Archbishop Kelly and Archbishop Smith to come forward to receive from you your gifts for their Provinces.

One of the gifts we wish to present to you is also intensely personal. It concerns the life of 17th century Bartholomew Holzhauser. As you know, Holy Father, Fr. Holzhauser began his Institute for Secular Clergy in your home- town of Tittmoning, in a building which later became your family home. You speak of this in your own memoirs. In the 19th century, interest in Holzhauser revived. He was declared Venerable by your predecessor Leo XIII. This college, St Mary's Oscott, became imbued with the spirit of Holzhauser when the rector, Henry Parkinson (1896-1924) formed this house in that spirit. He played a major role in founding the Apostolic Union of Secular Clergy, for the mutual support of priests. He also led the students in a translation of the life of Bartholomew Holzhauser. We have prepared a special edition of that text and we hope that it will remind you that the spirit of Holzhauser is still deeply formative in this house. ∎

Pope Benedict's Address at Oscott College

Oscott College, Birmingham, Sunday 19th September 2010. 5:40pm

My dear Brother Bishops,

This has been a day of great joy for the Catholic community in these islands. Blessed John Henry Newman, as we may now call him, has been raised to the altars as an example of heroic faithfulness to the Gospel and an intercessor for the Church in this land that he loved and served so well. Here in this very chapel in 1852, he gave voice to the new confidence and vitality of the Catholic community in England and Wales after the restoration of the hierarchy, and his words could be applied equally to Scotland a quarter of a century later. His beatification today is a reminder of the Holy Spirit's continuing action in calling forth gifts of holiness from among the people of Great Britain, so that from east to west and from north to south, a perfect offering of praise and thanksgiving may be made to the glory of God's name.

I thank Cardinal O'Brien and Archbishop Nichols for their words and, in so doing, I am reminded how recently I was able to welcome all of you to Rome for the *Ad Limina* visits of your respective Episcopal Conferences. We spoke then about some of the challenges you face as you lead your people in faith, particularly regarding the urgent need to proclaim the Gospel afresh in a highly secularised environment. In the course of my visit it has become clear to me how deep a thirst there is among the British people for the Good News of Jesus Christ. You have been chosen by God to offer them the living water of the Gospel, encouraging them to place their hopes, not in the vain enticements of this world, but in the firm assurances of the next. As you proclaim the coming of the Kingdom, with its promise of hope for the poor and the needy, the sick and the elderly, the unborn and the neglected, be sure to present in its fullness the life-giving message

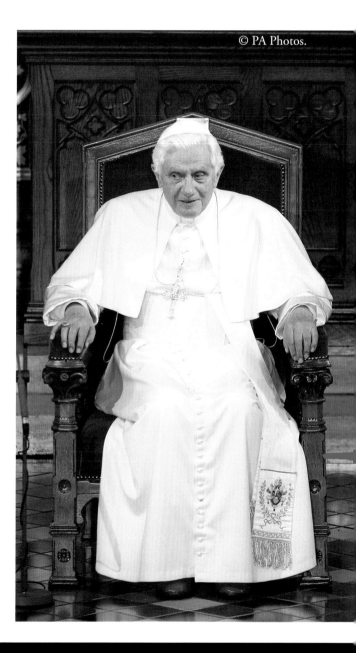

© PA Photos.

"O that God would grant the clergy to feel their weakness as sinful men, and the people to sympathise with them and love them and pray for their increase in all good gifts of grace."
Blessed John Henry Newman (Sermon, 22nd March 1829)

of the Gospel, including those elements which call into question the widespread assumptions of today's culture. As you know, a Pontifical Council has recently been established for the New Evangelisation of countries of long-standing Christian tradition, and I would encourage you to avail yourselves of its services in addressing the task before you. Moreover, many of the new ecclesial movements have a particular charism for evangelisation, and I know that you will continue to explore appropriate and effective ways of involving them in the mission of the Church.

Since your visit to Rome, political changes in the United Kingdom have focused attention on the consequences of the financial crisis, which has caused so much hardship to countless individuals and families. The spectre of unemployment is casting its shadow over many people's lives, and the long-term cost of the ill-advised investment practices of recent times is becoming all too evident. In these circumstances, there will be additional calls on the characteristic generosity of British Catholics, and I know that you will take a lead in calling for solidarity with those in need. The prophetic voice of Christians has an important role in highlighting the needs of the poor and disadvantaged, who can so easily be overlooked in the allocation of limited

resources. In their teaching document Choosing the Common Good, the bishops of England and Wales underlined the importance of the practice of virtue in public life. Today's circumstances provide a good opportunity to reinforce that message, and indeed to encourage people to aspire to higher moral values in every area of their lives, against a background of growing cynicism regarding even the possibility of virtuous living.

Another matter which has received much attention in recent months, and which seriously undermines the moral credibility of Church leaders, is the shameful abuse of children and young people by priests and religious. I have spoken on many occasions of the deep wounds that such behaviour causes, in the victims first and foremost, but also in the relationships of trust that should exist between priests and people, between priests and their bishops, and between the Church authorities and the public. I know that you have taken serious steps to remedy this situation, to ensure that children are effectively protected from harm and to deal properly and transparently with allegations as they arise. You have publicly acknowledged your deep regret over what has happened, and the often inadequate ways it was addressed in the past. Your growing awareness of the extent of child abuse in society, its devastating effects, and

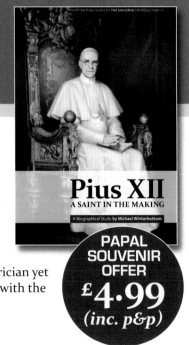

© Mazur/www.thepapalvisit.org.uk

the need to provide proper victim support should serve as an incentive to share the lessons you have learned with the wider community. Indeed, what better way could there be of making reparation for these sins than by reaching out, in a humble spirit of compassion, towards children who continue to suffer abuse elsewhere? Our duty of care towards the young demands nothing less.

As we reflect on the human frailty that these tragic events so starkly reveal, we are reminded that, if we >

Pope Benedict urged Scottish, English and Welsh bishops to give people real spiritual nourishment, not just easy or popular answers to their questions and doubts.

The British bishops have been criticised by some conservative Catholic commentators for an apparently lukewarm reception of provisions Pope Benedict made last year that would allow for the establishment of special Church jurisdictions for former Anglicans who want to maintain some of their Anglican heritage and practices.

The jurisdictions, known as ordinariates, have not yet been established anywhere in the world.

Some people involved in efforts to promote full Anglican-Roman Catholic unity said the Pope's special provisions were essentially an admission that full unity was virtually impossible because of the ordination of women priests and bishops and positions on homosexuality in some parts of the Anglican Communion.

The Rev. David Richardson, director of the Anglican Centre in Rome and the Archbishop of Canterbury's representative to the Vatican, said the idea of the ordinariate was initially billed as a "pastoral provision" for disaffected Anglicans and appears to offer benefits to them, but "seems to contribute nothing to the full visible unity" of the Anglican and Roman Catholic communities as a whole.

Full unity can only be achieved through formal dialogue between the Roman Catholic Church and the Anglican Communion as a whole, Rev. Richardson said. ∎

are to be effective Christian leaders, we must live lives of the utmost integrity, humility and holiness. As Blessed John Henry Newman once wrote, "O that God would grant the clergy to feel their weakness as sinful men, and the people to sympathise with them and love them and pray for their increase in all good gifts of grace" *(Sermon, 22nd March 1829)*. I pray that among the graces of this visit will be a renewed dedication on the part of Christian leaders to the prophetic vocation they have received, and a new appreciation on the part of the people for the great gift of the ordained ministry. Prayer for vocations will then arise spontaneously, and we may be confident that the Lord will respond by sending labourers to bring in the plentiful harvest that he has prepared throughout the United Kingdom *(cf. Mt 9:37-38)*. In this regard, I am glad that I will shortly have the opportunity to meet the seminarians of England, Scotland and Wales, and to assure them of my prayers as they prepare to play their part in bringing in that harvest.

Finally, I should like to speak to you about two specific matters that affect your episcopal ministry at this time. One is the imminent publication of the new translation of the Roman Missal. I want to take this opportunity to thank all of you for the contribution you have made, with such painstaking care, to the collegial exercise of reviewing and approving the texts. This has provided an immense service to Catholics throughout the English-speaking world. I encourage you now to seize the opportunity that the new translation offers for in-depth catechesis on the Eucharist and renewed devotion in the manner of its celebration. "The more lively the Eucharistic faith of the people of God, the deeper is its sharing in ecclesial life in steadfast commitment to the mission entrusted by Christ to his disciples" *(Sacramentum Caritatis, 6)*. The other matter I touched upon in February with the bishops of England and Wales, when I asked you to be generous in implementing the Apostolic Constitution Anglicanorum Coetibus. This should be seen as a prophetic gesture that can contribute positively to the developing relations between Anglicans and Catholics. It helps us to set our sights on the ultimate goal of all ecumenical activity: the restoration of full ecclesial communion in the context of which the mutual exchange of gifts from our respective spiritual patrimonies serves as an enrichment to us all. Let us continue to pray and work unceasingly in order to hasten the joyful day when that goal can be accomplished.

With these sentiments, I thank you warmly for your hospitality over the past four days. Commending all of you and the people you serve to the intercession of St Andrew, St David and St George, I am pleased to impart my Apostolic Blessing to you and to all the clergy, religious and lay faithful of England, Scotland and Wales. ■

© Mazur/www.thepapalvisit.org.uk

TREASURE EVERY MOMENT
OF THE HOLY FATHER'S VISIT FOREVER

The Royal Mint

Pope Benedict XVI's four day visit to the UK, from 16th – 19th September, will be a momentous occasion for all UK Catholics. To help you celebrate, The Royal Mint has created a range of official medals that will provide an ever-lasting memory of this historic occasion.

The front of the medal features a beautiful image of Pope Benedict XVI. The reverse shows the Papal insignia of the Keys to Heaven and Earth, surrounded by the wording "The Papal Visit to the UK 2010".

The Official 2010 Papal Visit Medal: **£10.00**

Alloy: Nickel-brass   Weight: 28.28g
Diameter: 38.45mm   Maximum Medal Mintage: 50,000
Obverse and reverse designer: Gordon Summers

also available in **Silver** £45.00

Alloy: 0.925Ag   Maximum Medal Mintage: 6,000

Medal pack

Silver Medal

2010
HEART
SPEAKS
UNTO HEART

Prime Minister David Cameron's speech to Pope Benedict XVI

Birmingham International Airport, Sunday 19th September 2010. 6:30pm

Your Holiness Pope Benedict, Your Excellencies, Ladies and Gentlemen. This ceremony brings to a close an incredibly moving four days for our country.

Your Holiness, on this truly historic first State Visit to Britain you have spoken to a nation of six million Catholics but you have been heard by a nation of more than 60 million citizens and by many millions more all around the world.

For you have offered a message not just to the Catholic Church but to each and every one of us of every faith and none.

A challenge to us all to follow our conscience to ask not what are my entitlements, but what are my responsibilities? To ask not what we can do for ourselves, but what we can do for others?

Cardinal Newman, who was beatified here in Birmingham this morning, once said that one little deed whether by someone who helps "to relieve the sick and needy" or someone who "forgives an enemy" evinces more true faith than could be shown by "the most fluent religious conversation or the most intimate knowledge of Scripture."

In his immense contribution to the philosophy of higher education, Cardinal Newman reminded the world of the need for education for life not just for the workplace.

That broader education for life mattered because of the responsibilities of each person in society obligations and opportunities that came from what

Cardinal Newman described as the "common bond of unity" that we all share.

Your Holiness, this common bond has been an incredibly important part of your message to us.

And it's at the heart of the new culture of social responsibility we want to build in Britain.

People of faith – including our 30,000 faith-based charities – are great architects of that new culture.

For many, faith is a spur to action. It shapes their beliefs and behaviour; and it gives them a sense of purpose. Crucially, it is their faith that inspires them to help others.

And we should celebrate that.

Faith is part of the fabric of our country. It always has been and it always will be.

As you, your Holiness, have said, faith is not a problem for legislators to solve but rather a vital part of our national conversation.

And we are proud of that.

But people do not have to share a religious faith or agree with religion on everything to see the benefit of asking the searching questions that you, your Holiness, have posed to us about our society and how we treat ourselves and each other.

You have really challenged the whole country to sit up and think, and that can only be a good thing.

Because I believe we can all share in your message of working for the common good and that we all have a social obligation each other, to our families and our communities.

And, of course, our obligations to each other – and our care for each other – must extend beyond these shores too.

Your Holiness, in our meeting yesterday and in the discussions with the papal delegation on Friday evening we agreed to develop the co-operation between this country and the Holy See on the key international issues where we share a common goal.

On winning the argument to get to grips with climate change.

On promoting a multi-faith dialogue and working for peace in our world

On fighting poverty and disease.

I passionately believe that we must continue to help the poorest, even in difficult economic times.

A yawning gap between the rich and the poor will be more dangerous and less secure for all of us.

© PA Photos.

So this country will keep its promises on aid.

We will work to hold other countries to their keep promises too.

And to make sure that money we spend on aid goes to those who need it most.

And I am delighted that the Holy See will be working so actively with us to do all we can to achieve this.

Your Holiness, your presence here has been a great honour for our country.

Now you are leaving us – and I hope with strong memories.

When you think of our country, think of it as one that not only cherishes faith, but one that is deeply, but quietly, compassionate.

I see it in the incredible response to the floods in Pakistan.

I see it in the spirit of community that drives countless good deeds done for friends and neighbours every day.

And in my own life, I have seen it in the many, many kind messages that I have had as I have cradled a new daughter and said goodbye to a wonderful father.

As we stand here in Birmingham to bid you farewell, let me return to the words of Cardinal Newman.

The Cardinal is greatly remembered here in Birmingham for his care for its people. During a cholera outbreak in the city, he worked tirelessly among the poor and sick.

And when he himself died, the poor of the city turned out in their thousands to line the streets. Inscribed on the pall of his coffin, was his motto **"Heart speaks unto heart".** That has been the theme of this most special visit.

I hope it is a reflection of the welcome that you have received. It is most definitely a fitting tribute to the words you have spoken and the sentiments that you leave behind.

I wish you and your delegation a safe return to Rome.

And I look forward to ever closer co-operation between the UK and the Holy See as we redouble our resolve to work for the common good, both here in Britain and with our partners abroad. ∎

© **Prime Minister's Office**

Pope Benedict XVI's farewell address at Birmingham Airport

Birmingham International Airport, Sunday 19th September 2010. 6:45pm

© PA Photos.

Prime Minister,

Thank you for your kind words of farewell on behalf of Her Majesty's Government and the people of the United Kingdom. I am very grateful for all the hard work of preparation, on the part of both the present and the previous Government, the civil service, local authorities and police, and the many volunteers who patiently helped to prepare for the events of these four days. Thank you for the warmth of your welcome and for the hospitality that I have enjoyed.

During my time with you, I have been able to meet representatives of the many communities, cultures, languages and religions that make up British society. The very diversity of modern Britain is a challenge to its Government and people, but it also represents a great opportunity to further intercultural and interreligious dialogue for the enrichment of the entire community.

>

In these days, I was grateful for the opportunity to meet Her Majesty the Queen, as well as yourself and other political leaders, and to be able to discuss matters of common interest, both at home and abroad. I was particularly honoured to be invited to address both Houses of Parliament in the historic precincts of Westminster Hall. I sincerely hope that these occasions will contribute to confirming and strengthening the excellent relations between the Holy See and the United Kingdom, especially in co-operation for international development, in care for the natural environment, and in the building of a civil society with a renewed sense of shared values and common purpose.

It was also my pleasure to visit His Grace the Archbishop of Canterbury and the Bishops of the Church of England, and later to pray with them and our fellow Christians in the evocative surroundings of Westminster Abbey, a place which speaks so eloquently of our shared traditions and culture. As Britain is home to so many religious traditions, I was grateful to have the opportunity to meet their representatives and to share some thoughts with them about the contribution that the religions can offer to the development of a healthy pluralistic society.

Naturally, my visit was directed in a special way to the Catholics of the United Kingdom. I treasure the time spent with the bishops, clergy, religious and laity, and with teachers, pupils and older people. It was especially moving to celebrate with them, here in Birmingham, the beatification of a great son of England, Cardinal John Henry Newman. With his vast legacy of scholarly and spiritual writings, I am certain that he still has much to teach us about Christian living and witness amid the challenges of today's world, challenges which he foresaw with such remarkable clarity.

As I take my leave of you, let me assure you once again of my good wishes and prayers for the peace and prosperity of Great Britain. Thank you very much and God bless you all! ■

Pope Benedict XVI waves as he boards his aircraft at Birmingham International Airport on the last day of his State visit to the UK. ©PA Photos.

STONYHURST

Leading Catholic boarding and day school community in the Jesuit ethos for girls and boys 3–18

Open Days

St Mary's Hall – 3-13 year olds (Nursery - Year 8)
Saturday 16 October

College – for 13+ and 16+ entry (Year 9-13)
Saturday 6 November

To find out more and to receive your invitation please contact the Admissions office

Stonyhurst Clitheroe Lancashire BB7 9PZ

T 01254 827073 / 9   F 01254 827135   admissions@stonyhurst.ac.uk

www.stonyhurst.ac.uk